ÉTIENNE DE LA BOÉTIE

Discourse on Voluntary Servitude

ÉTIENNE DE LA BOÉTIE

Discourse on Voluntary Servitude

Translated by
James B. Atkinson *&* David Sices

Introduction and Notes by
James B. Atkinson

Hackett Publishing Company, Inc.
Indianapolis/Cambridge

15 14 13 12   1 2 3 4 5 6 7

For further information, please address
Hackett Publishing Company, Inc.
P.O. Box 44937
Indianapolis, Indiana 46244-0937

www.hackettpublishing.com

Interior design and composition by Elizabeth L. Wilson
Printed at Data Reproductions Corporation

Library of Congress Cataloging-in-Publication Data
La Boétie, Estienne de, 1530–1563.
  [De la servitude volontaire. English]
  Discourse on voluntary servitude / Étienne La Boétie ; translated by James B.
Atkinson and David Sices ; introduction and notes by James B. Atkinson.
    p.   cm.
  "This translation is based on Estienne de La Boétie, De la servitude volontaire ou
Contr'un, edited by Malcolm Smith, with additional annotation and a bibliography
by Michel Magnien (Geneva: Librarie Droz, 2001)" — Publisher.
  Includes bibliographical references and index.
  ISBN 978-1-60384-839-8 (pbk.) — ISBN 978-1-60384-840-4 (cloth)
  1. Political science—Early works to 1800. 2. Liberty. I. Atkinson, James B., 1934–
II. Sices, David. IV. Title.
  JC139.L1513 2012
  320.01'1—dc23   2012019676

Contents

INTRODUCTION

Recently, theatergoers in Avignon were able to attend a philosophical monologue "hosted" by an actor playing Michel de Montaigne. The stage set was such that he graciously invited the audience to partake of his hospitality and to share his appetite for ideas, reflections, and musings. Later in the year the play was restaged in Limoges, but the audience there had another choice. They could also spend an evening with an actor, on a stage set reminiscent of a Samuel Beckett play, in the role of La Boétie urging the audience to refuse servitude: "Resolve no longer to be slaves and you are free!" The speech and stage presence of both a Montaigne and a La Boétie all in one town, in one week—that would have been a sight to behold.

Theatrically speaking, however, La Boétie appears to have been rather upstaged—an afterthought, as he so often is. History has doomed him to a shadowy existence. Montaigne casts one shadow. Depending on the viewer's perspective, or seat in the audience, La Boétie can be either solidly in view—a forceful and unmistakable presence—or, as King Lear's fool might put it, "an O without a figure." A wag might go even further and borrow a gibe from Robert Louis Stevenson: "I have a little shadow that goes in and out with me, / And what can be the use of him is more than I can see." Perhaps, from the point of view of Montaigne studies, La Boétie's shadow does go in and out of focus so often that its use is not immediately clear. And then, there is the shadow La Boétie casts through the enigmatic *Discourse on Voluntary Servitude*. Despite these shadows' knack for elusion, the scholars would be well served to sharpen their vision, both to see La Boétie himself more distinctly and to deepen our understanding of the puzzling figure of Montaigne as well. Certainly La Boétie's *Discourse on Voluntary Servitude (or Against One)* deserves to be brought further into the light.

La Boétie: An Emerging Portrait

But, for the moment, let's concentrate on forming a sharper image of La Boétie, someone who epitomizes what we think of as a "Renaissance man." A more distinct picture, based primarily on literary evidence, would provide an opportunity to see La Boétie more clearly—even if the primary form of evidence, Montaigne's writings, make Montaigne's shadow ultimately inescapable. But we need not let this web of shadows define La Boétie. We can strive to create a picture of La Boétie through this web. To extend the visual metaphors, it is a proper scholarly portrait that La Boétie lacks, and here we might resort to a device similar to one Montaigne used almost five centuries ago. In introducing La Boétie to his own readers in his essay "Friendship," Montaigne laments that his "ability does not reach so far as to dare undertake a rich, polished picture, shaped according to art." Nevertheless, Montaigne plunges right ahead with one, setting a standard for subsequent essays describing the ideal friendship—one "so complete and so perfect . . . that it would be a great thing were fortune to achieve it once in three centuries." But is Montaigne's "polished picture" of his friend really "so complete"? It would be no exaggeration to say that this portrait helped create La Boétie's shadowy legacy: Montaigne's comments, after all, are the primary contemporary source available to us.

As portraits go, then, this one warrants further attention; I want to bring La Boétie out of this shadow. If Montaigne can enlist the rhetorical principle of preterition in his essay, boldly proceeding to do what he announces he is unable to do, perhaps it is worth risking an attempt to do the same. To arrive at a final portrait, one that results in La Boétie appearing clearly before our eyes, we need to sketch out his external appearance and attributes, add touches suggestive of his character, and fill in his main features but shade them slightly to achieve a portrait in which Montaigne is, at best, but a pentimento.

A preparatory portrait sketch of Étienne de La Boétie's life might begin by noting that he shared more than friendship with Michel de Montaigne—his background was quite similar as well. Essential to the public lives of both men was service in the Bordeaux *Parlement*. Armed with substantial legal training, its magistrates dovetailed with the class of wealthy merchants to rule the town's political and cultural activity. The *Parlement*, the highest court of justice in all France and hence a key element of the king's judicial power, was composed of eight regional members, of which the one in Bordeaux was the fourth oldest; these *Parlements* were responsible for local laws and administering royal justice throughout the country. A rapport with the king was an essential part of the magistrates' ability to function—magistrates were charged with dispensing royal proclamations, among other things, even if they frequently took issue with them. If the king himself were to be rendered ineffective, as happened during the Wars of Religion in the second half of the sixteenth century, the *Parlement* stepped in and set policy. These wars, of course, darkened the lives and works of both La Boétie and Montaigne, in and out of *Parlement*; they did not end until the Peace of Alais in 1629. The Bordeaux *Parlement* that La Boétie entered in 1554 was a rather intricate establishment. It had several chambers: a "short-lived Requêtes [that heard petitions] . . . two Chambres des Enquêtes [inquiry] reporting, with only primary jurisdiction, on civil cases up for appeal; the Grand' Chambre, or Chamber of Pleas, which judged these cases; and the Tournelle, filled in rotation by members of the other chambers, which sat on criminal cases."[1] In addition to their position in the *Parlement*, both men shared a common geographical background: they lived near one another in Gascogne, a region so famous for its proud heritage that the word *gasconade* entered English as a synonym for boasting.

La Boétie was born on November 1, 1530, in Sarlat-la-Canéda, a scenic town on the Cuze River not far north of the Dordogne River and about fifty miles from where Montaigne would be born almost two and a half years later. La Boétie's father was an admired civil servant, and his mother's brother was a president of the Bordeaux *Parlement*. Both of La Boétie's parents died when he was ten. He was fortunate to have been brought up by a namesake uncle, Étienne de La Boétie, his godfather and curate of Bouilhonnas, who was devoted to theological and legal studies as well as to antiquity and was determined that his nephew would follow suit. In fact, Montaigne quotes

---

1. Frame, *Montaigne*, p. 49. See "Suggestions for Further Reading" for full bibliographic information for this and subsequent notes.

La Boétie on his deathbed praising his uncle: "I have always said that everything a very wise, a very good, and a very liberal father could do for his son, all of that you have done for me, whether in the attention necessary to instruct me in humane letters or when you were pleased to launch me into public service . . . in short, whatever I have, I acknowledge that I got from you, I am beholden to you for it; you are my true father."[2]

With a deeply engrained respect for letters, La Boétie pursued the requisite humanistic curriculum of his day, though it is impossible to specify whether he did so in Bordeaux at the Collège de Guyenne, where Montaigne studied, or in Toulouse; he was briefly in Paris, where he first came in contact with members of what would become the Pléiade, a group of French poets—about which more later. He studied canon and civil law at the University of Orléans, which was in the forefront of legal education, on a par with the University of Bologna. Both institutions eschewed the scholastic approach to jurisprudence and replaced it with the tools of Renaissance humanists: philology and a study of past precedents. In September of 1553 he completed his study in Orléans, where free inquiry was particularly emphasized; some of its faculty members and students were not Catholics, adherents of the dominant religion in France, but Calvinists who encouraged free inquiry both from a religious and educational viewpoint. Renowned European legal scholars at Orléans included the jurist Charles Dumoulin (1500–1566) and La Boétie's professor Anne du Bourg (b. 1521), who was hanged and his body burned for his Calvinist pronouncements in 1559.

Upon receiving his degree in 1553, La Boétie so impressed his peers that, on the recommendation of the Orléans faculty, King Henri II issued letters patent that sent him from Orléans to Bordeaux. The king also ordered Guillaume de Lur, known also as Guillaume de Longa (as well as Lur-Longa), to hand over his position as magistrate in the Bordeaux *Parlement* to La Boétie; in turn, the king appointed Lur-Longa to the Paris *Parlement*. The fact that La Boétie was under legal age for the position in Bordeaux—he was only twenty-two, not the requisite twenty-five—indicates the high

---

2. La B made this admission as he was dying; M heard it and quoted it in a letter to his father; Pléiade 1, pp. 1351–52.

degree of respect for his talent and potential. Lur-Longa, who will prove relevant to our eventual understanding of the *Discourse on Voluntary Servitude*,³ had established a distinguished record as a magistrate in Bordeaux and was associated with such Bordeaux humanists at the Collège de Guyenne as George Buchanan, professor of Latin. (Montaigne referred to this teacher of his as a "skilled craftsman" in the "trade" of poetry, and was proud of playing the "main part" in one of Buchanan's Latin tragedies.) Given these perhaps unfamiliar names—Charles Dumoulin, Anne du Bourg, Lur-Longa, and Buchanan—all of whom became associated with or espoused reformist ideas, we catch our first glimpse of how some readers might come to exploit La Boétie's *Discourse on Voluntary Servitude* later in the sixteenth century. (Buchanan eventually aligned himself with a group of French Protestants called the Monarchomachs—literally, "fighters against monarchs"—who argued on behalf of popular sovereignty.

It is generally assumed that in the interim between learning of his appointment and assuming his duties in May of 1554, La Boétie selected his wife from this circle of educated humanists in Bordeaux, someone from a family that was also well connected in local politics. Marguerite de Carle, whose brother was president of the Bordeaux *Parlement*, was a widow with a son and a daughter who later married Montaigne's eldest brother, Thomas. Since her daughter was fifteen years younger than La Boétie, it is safe to assume that Marguerite de Carle was a bit older than her husband. Biographers seem to agree that, though little is in fact known about her, Marguerite's marriage to La Boétie was a happy one.

Throughout his brief life (he died in 1563), La Boétie's activities combined interest in literature and translation with a commitment to public service. His devotion to the former resulted from his humanistic training, of course, but it is important to remember that he published nothing while he was alive. Montaigne assumed the

3. Trinquet, *Jeunesse de Montaigne*, pp. 565, 612, suggests that Lur-Longa may have been the person M alluded to when he says in "Friendship," I, 28 [27], about La B's work: "it was shown to me long before I met him and made me first aware of his name" (Montaigne, *Selected Essays*, ed. Atkinson and Sices, p. 74; hereafter cited as *Selected Essays*). Magnien, in the Smith-Magnien edition, p. 100, suggests La B may even have thought of Lur-Longa as a father figure.

responsibility for getting his works into print, but, as we shall see, what he omitted is more significant than what he included.[4] While modern studies concentrate less on La Boétie's poetry than his prose, his contemporaries were quite familiar with his verse. Members of the Pléiade, a group of French Renaissance poets who advocated using classical poetic forms in the vernacular—in the words of their spokesman, Joachim Du Bellay, "to illustrate the French language"—praised La Boétie's Latin, and especially his French, poetry. Montaigne, too, thought highly of the latter: "since he wrote them in his greenest youth, inflamed with a fine, noble passion," La Boétie's vernacular poems had "an indescribable liveliness and ebullience" about them.[5] While they display the rather conventional emotions of the love poetry then in vogue and are often stiff and bookish as well,[6] one senses in them an admirable empathy for humanity. At any rate, Montaigne made sure that twenty-nine of La Boétie's love poems were published in 1580. They immediately followed his essay "Friendship" in all the five editions of the *Essays* published during Montaigne's lifetime;[7] their place in modern editions, however, is replaced with only his dedicatory letter for La

---

4. One work "omitted" is something he allegedly wrote, but that no one has ever been able to locate: In 1768, in an updated edition of his *Bibliothèque historique de la France*, Jacques Le Long noted that Simon Millanges, who published the first edition of M's *Essays* in 1580, also published *Histoirique description du solitaire et sauvage pays de Médoc (dans le Bordelois), par feu M. De La Boétie* in 1593 (Bonnefon, p. 398). In 1578 Millanges also brought out a forerunner of Milton's *Paradise Lost*, the poem *La Sepmaine; ou, Création du monde* by the Huguenot writer Guillaume de Salluste Du Bartas (1544–1590).

5. "Twenty-Nine Sonnets by Étienne de La Boétie," I, 29 [28], dedicatory letter to Diane d'Andoins, countess de Guiche and de Grammont; Pléiade 1, p. 194; Pléiade 2, p. 202; V-S, p. 196.

6. Admittedly this judgment echoes what many of his contemporaries thought. For a different outlook, see Malcolm Quainton, "Vers François . . . Pas Assez Limez Pour Estre Mis en Lumiere," in Tetel (ed.), *Étienne de La Boétie*, pp. 89–104, and Françoise Charpentier, "Les Poésies Françaises d'Étienne de La Boétie," also in Tetel, pp. 105–19.

7. For their absence in editions after 1588, see Michel Magnien, "De l'hyperbole à l'ellipse: Montaigne face aux sonnets de La Boétie," *Montaigne Studies: An Interdisciplinary Forum* 2, no. 1 (September 1990): 7–25.

Boétie's twenty-nine sonnets. Toward the end of his life, Montaigne sought to get several of his deceased friend's works published, thereby promoting someone who "lived his whole life, stagnating and belittled, by the ashes of his family hearth."[8] This same letter conveys his bitter resentment at his generation's failure to acknowledge fully La Boétie's unimpeachable character and his literary accomplishments, not merely in his Latin poems:

> what was most admirable in him, the true juice and marrow of his worth, have followed him, and what is left for us is bark and leaves. [A man] who could enable us to see the disciplined impulses of his soul, his piety, his virtue, his justness, the readiness of his mind, the weight and soundness of his judgment, the loftiness of his conceptions—so far above those of ordinary people—his learning, the graciousness that was the usual companion of his actions, the tender love he bore for his abject country, his mortal and sworn hatred for all vice, but particularly for that sordid traffic concocted under the honorable title of justice: such a man would surely breed in all good men an uncommon affection for him, mingled with an amazing sadness at his loss.

Palpable is both Montaigne's rancor and his reverence.

La Boétie's literary activity also included translations of poetry and prose.[9] As a gift for Marguerite de Carle, he translated selections from some of Bradamante's grief and lamentations in Canto 32 of Ariosto's mock epic *Orlando Furioso* (1532). (Though there is little likelihood that it had anything to do with La Boétie's choice of verses from this poem, Ariosto sometimes refers through metonymy to Bradamante, because of her lineage, as "the lady of Dordogne"—an epithet La Boétie might have intended as

---

8. His *fouyer domestique*; see the Dedicatory Letter for La B's Latin poems written to Michel de l'Hôpital in 1570; Pléiade 1, pp. 1363–64.

9. For the following discussion of La B's translations, four essays, all in Tetel, *Étienne de La Boétie*, have been useful: Michel Magnien, "La Boétie traducteur des anciens," pp. 15–44; John O'Brien, "De l'*Oeconomicus* à *La Mesnagerie*: La Boétie et Xénophon," pp. 45–62; Alessandra Preda, "Les enjeux de la traduction de l'Arioste," pp. 63–86; and Perrine Galand-Hallyn, "Les 'Essais' Latins d'Étienne de la Boétie (*Poemata*, 1571)": 121–56.

an allusion to Marguerite de Carle herself—and even as "the valiant lady of Dordogne."[10]) La Boétie addresses the preface to these selections, also in verse, to his wife and incorporates a statement about his theory of translation. In tune with the new trend in poetry heralded by the Pléiade, he emphasizes the primacy of the poet's ability to invent over merely being a "turner of phrases." In his prose translations he demonstrated his proficiency in Greek by translating Xenophon's *Oeconomicus* (whose title is the root of our word *economy*), a Socratic dialogue on estate and household management, tasks with which many people, then and now, begin their encounter with the basic principles of economy. Two other translations from the Greek were from Plutarch's moral treatises: "Advice to Bride and Groom" (*Moralia* 2, 138a–146a) in which, despite the note of deference recommended for a wife, there is a strong emphasis on companionship and mutual respect; and "Letter of Consolation to His Wife" (*Moralia* 7, 608b–612b), in which he deals with the death of their two-year-old daughter. The letter's personal cast was so touching that, centuries later, Montaigne turned to it for solace when his two-month-old daughter died, presenting it to his wife Françoise de La Chassigne, confident that La Boétie's version of Plutarch could console her "much better than" any expression of his own "intentions."[11] Finally, La Boétie helped a member of the Bordeaux *Parlement*, the eminent French jurist Arnoul Le Ferron, establish the Greek text for Plutarch's "Dialogue on Love," his *Erotikos* or *Amatorius* (*Moralia* 9, 748e–771e), so that Le Ferron could translate it into Latin.[12]

---

10. In this case the Dordogne refers to the region, now a department in southwestern France east of Bordeaux, through which flows the Dordogne River, one of France's major rivers. Gascogne-Gascony, referred to earlier, is part of this area.

11. This dedicatory letter was dated September 10, 1570; Pléiade 1, p. 1371. Unfortunately, M referred to the death of his "two-year," not "two-month," old daughter; critics have offered various explanations—none very satisfactory—ranging from a printer's error to oversight, though in his *Ephemeris*, a personal register-like diary, he listed her birth accurately, June of 1570, and her death "two months later"; Pléiade 1, p. 1407.

12. In gratitude for his expertise in working on the Greek text, Le Ferron referred admiringly to La B as an "Attic man"; see Magnien, "La Boétie traducteur des anciens," in Tetel, *Étienne de La Boétie*, p. 23.

With the exception of the "letter of consolation," it has been argued that there is a consistency to the Greek texts La Boétie chose to translate. They suggest an interest in management that is in line with the *Discourse on Voluntary Servitude* and its claim that the proper administration of the state ought to mirror that of the home. Magnien believes that his translations of Greek successfully "transfer," from the literal meaning of *translatio*, the text into expressive French, thereby furthering Du Bellay's goal of "illustrating" the French language—that is, showing the brilliance of the language—and putting La Boétie in the advance guard of his day. He also remarks on the consistency of La Boétie's translating choices: though they relate thematically to the joys of hearth and home, subjects Montaigne described as La Boétie's *fouyer domestique*, Montaigne saw them in the negative light of the "ashes of his family hearth" where La Boétie lived belittled and in stagnation.[13]

La Boétie's scholarly work with Le Ferron indicates that his legal and political career was also dependent on the pervasive humanist culture he had imbued since childhood. He performed his duties conscientiously in the Bordeaux *Parlement* where, during his first six years, he seems to have been primarily involved with local issues. While only five of the cases Montaigne worked on have survived, we have twenty-two of those La Boétie drafted: "It seems quite clear that La Boétie took to the work of the *Parlement* more than did his friend."[14]

Primary among the immediate problems La Boétie faced were those connected with the increased tension between Catholics and Huguenots, a nickname originally given to French Protestants who followed the reforms of John Calvin and ultimately formed the Protestant Reformed Church of France. The *Parlement*, asserting loyalty to the king and claiming the restoration of order, consistently ruled against Protestants: for example, they condemned a Protestant minister to death, burned at the stake two men accused of heresy and a man accused of defacing statues of Mary and of Jesus, and finally, in 1560, denied Huguenots the right to assemble.

---

13. Magnien, "La Boétie traducteur des anciens," in Tetel, *Étienne de La Boétie*, p. 39.

14. Frame, *Montaigne*, p. 57.

In December of 1560, though, La Boétie was sent on a mission to the royal counsel in Paris, ostensibly to deal with a question of salary payments for the Bordeaux magistrates but actually to discuss the growing danger of open civil strife between the Huguenots and Catholics not only in southwest France, where it was virulent, but throughout the country. The date is important because this was a delicate moment in French history. The ensuing decade, characterized by a weak monarchy and a depressed economy, was rife with internecine rivalry among various political and religious groups. Henri II, who had succeeded his brilliant, powerful father François I in 1547, died in July of 1559. Henri's fifteen-year-old son François II reigned briefly before dying of tuberculosis, then his ten-year-old brother became Charles IX in 1560 and kept the throne until 1574. But Henri's wife, Catherine de' Medici acted as regent and dominated the reign of these two kings. She confronted three rapacious family factions struggling for power in a situation they considered ripe for realizing their private ambitions: the Protestant Bourbon princes, especially Louis I de Bourbon, prince de Condé; the Catholic Montmorencys; and the Guises, with whom she eventually forged a tenuous alliance. Her power was constantly threatened, requiring complicated and perpetual accommodation between personal aspirations and religious principles. Such accommodations, then, would occupy the legal career of La Boétie as well.

While in Paris La Boétie met Michel de L'Hôpital, an enlightened statesman whom Catherine de' Medici had recently appointed chancellor of France. Mutual respect gradually developed into a friendship, one strengthened by La Boétie's initial investment in L'Hôpital's strategies regarding the religion issue.[15] Upon his return to Bordeaux, he spoke in the *Parlement* on behalf of L'Hôpital's policy of conciliation toward Catholics and Protestants. Later, from September to December of 1561, having been sent to the Agenais (the area around Agen, a city about seventy-five miles southeast of Bordeaux) to accompany the king's representative, the chevalier de Coucy, Monsieur de Burie, La Boétie saw for himself the disappointing results of L'Hôpital and de' Medici's accommodations, however noble the effort to resolve the region's religious tensions.

---

15. This respect prompted M to dedicated his publication of La B's Latin verse in 1570 to Michel de L'Hôpital.

This experience caused him to doubt his original position, though he found the attempts to mollify both sides to be impressive. These attempts were motivated by beliefs outlined in a speech Michel de L'Hôpital gave in December of 1560, the same month La Boé-tie arrived in Paris. L'Hôpital declared, "It is folly to hope for peace, repose, and friendship among people of different faiths."[16] L'Hôpital recognized that political unity and religious unity were interdependent. One "lure" to try to bring about a meeting of minds was a compromise in the form of an edict, promulgated in January of 1562, which granted Protestants more freedom of worship—for example, those around Bordeaux and other French towns could worship openly in the suburbs. Of course, because they had to continue to worship privately when they were *in* town, such a concession satisfied neither party in the end. The massacre of a group of worshiping Huguenots by a party led by François de Guise prompted L'Hôpital's decision. Later that year, concerned that the government's position was in fact overly tolerant and perhaps reflecting his disheartening experience in the Agenais, La Boétie backed away from supporting the gesture in his critique: "Memoir Concerning the Edict of January 1562."[17] (Based on its first sentence, this work is sometimes referred to as "Memoir on the Pacification of the Troubles," which suits scholars who believe the essay was written in 1561; they prefer this title because they believe a specific event did not spark its composition.) He concluded that Protestant hopes for more freedom of worship should be dispatched resolutely, though without ill will. He continued to insist that Catholicism should be the official state religion, while acknowledging that it needed reform ("the Church [is] . . . astoundingly corrupt with infinite abuse"). Finally, he observed that civil strife might well destroy the entire country if nothing were done. Still, he decided that the king, not the Roman Catholic Church, should conceive and implement those reforms and if the Huguenots could not accept these changes, they should consider emigration.

---

16. As quoted in Bakewell, *How to Live, or, A Life of Montaigne in One Question and Twenty Attempts at an Answer*, p. 82.

17. Although it is generally accepted that La B wrote the "Memoir" because of its well-defined argument, Anne-Marie Cocula believes it was written by an anonymous cleric seeking to reform Catholicism; *Bulletin de la Société de Montaigne* 8th Series, no. 4 (July–December, 1996): 51–56.

La Boétie's "Memoir" had a rather curious fate. Though his loyalty, too, was decidedly on the Catholic side, Montaigne declined to publish it posthumously in 1570, when he released some of La Boétie's other works, because he found its "manner too delicate and refined to abandon . . . to the coarse and heavy air of so unpleasant a season"[18]—that is, the poisoned atmosphere of heightened religious strife. Thus Montaigne was responsible for the "Memoir" being lost for more than three centuries; it was not rediscovered and published until 1917.

There is a further shadow from the Montaigne family cast upon the furtive character of La Boétie: that of Michel de Montaigne's brother Thomas, who was sympathetic to Protestantism. This shadow clarifies La Boétie's thoughts about the Protestant-Catholic divide more fully. In a letter Montaigne wrote to his father about La Boétie's death, he quotes his friend's deathbed remarks to Thomas and especially his profound awareness that religious dissent could completely tear apart a person, a family, and a country:

> I swear to you that of all those who have taken up reformation of the Church, I have never thought there was any one person who went about it with better zeal, more complete, sincere, and simple affection than you. And I certainly believe that only the vices of our prelates, which are unquestionably in great need of correction, and some imperfections that time in its course has brought into our Church, have prompted you to this. At this point I do not want to wean you away from it now because I also do not willingly ask anyone to do something, whatever it might be, against his conscience. But, out of respect for [your family's] good reputation . . . a family as dear to me as any family in the world—My God, what a family, from which there has never issued any act other than one of a good man! . . . I certainly want to advise you . . . to shrink from these extremes. Do not be so intense and so violent; adapt yourself to these

---

18. There may well be some irony in the description of the "manner" being "too delicate and refined"; see Pléiade 1, p. 1719, from the "Notice to the Reader," August 10, 1570, which M appended to his edition of La B's translation of Xenophon's *Oeconomicus*.

extremes. Do not form a separate group or party; meet them. You see how much ruin these discords have brought into this kingdom, and I contend that they will bring even greater ones to it. And, since you are wise and good, refrain from placing these unseemly matters into your family's midst.[19]

Using family as metaphor for society, La Boétie effectively and succinctly makes his stance crystal clear—perhaps more directly than in the "Memoir Concerning the Edict of January 1562."

There are, of course, a few benefits to Montaigne's shadow extending over La Boétie, in that we learn more about the man through his better-documented friend. An incident centered on the Bordeaux *Parlement* occurred in 1563, the year La Boétie died, points out some of these benefits. The city's records and documents describing the situation quote Montaigne, so we know more about his role in the drama than La Boétie's, which should not be surprising, given the dearth of contemporary documents relative to La Boétie. As ever, it arose from religious strife. Mid-sixteenth-century Bordeaux was basically a Catholic city; Protestants made up only about 14 percent of its population. In 1563 the *Parlement*, under the leadership of First President Jacques Benoît de Lagebâton, sought—as it had habitually done—to maintain a moderate position. King Henri II considered him a trusted agent, and he was a friend, even a protégé, of Michel de L'Hôpital, from whom he derived his relatively lenient policy toward Protestant worship. Yet this policy caused dissension in the Bordeaux *Parlement*, and one Catholic leader, François de Péruse d'Escars, would challenge Lagebâton's right to govern in December of 1563. In his defense, Lagebâton named *Parlement* members who "often went to eat and drink with the sieur d'Escars, which made them contemptible, to the point where the sieur d'Escars sent for them at any time and used them on such negotiations as he pleased." Both La Boétie and Montaigne were among those the First President cited. While La Boétie was indeed visiting d'Escars when he contracted the disease that killed him in August of 1563, it is doubtful that he would have been in league with such an extreme partisan of the Catholic position; like Lagebâton, La Boétie adhered

---

19. As quoted in M's letter to his father seven years later, November 24, 1570; Pléiade 1, p. 1356.

to the more tolerant policies of his friend Michel de L'Hôpital. And Montaigne, according to the record—no doubt incensed that Lagebâton included among the "contemptible" the now dead La Boétie—"expressed himself with all the vivacity of his character, and said . . . that the First President was not qualified to offer to challenge anyone, by way of remonstrance or otherwise, when he himself was challenged."[20] To oppose Montaigne's right to be a magistrate in the *Parlement* was a serious charge; it cast a slur on his integrity and, more outrageously, on the character of his dead, defenseless friend. This incident represents a valuable, positive confirmation that neither man, despite friendship with d'Escars, thought of himself as blindly in another man's pocket. Both firmly believed their independence was inviolable.

Montaigne's literary shadow even lingers over La Boétie's death, on August 18, 1563, when he was only thirty-two years old. It takes the form of a poignant letter he wrote his father, the same one referred to in which he recreated the scene with Montaigne's brother, Thomas.[21] Contrary to modern expectations, a Renaissance letter was not always thought of as a private communication—the tone of Montaigne's, for example, clearly indicates that it was shaped for an audience, not his father alone and intended to display the author's literary craft and intellectual versatility. The public, literary cast to this particular letter—it almost sounds as if it were written as a funeral oration or even a saint's life—is clear because it reflects classical canons of hero worship and consolation; these elements are mingled with reconstructions of the dying man's speeches to family, friends (such as Thomas), and Montaigne, whom he often held by the hand.

Most scholars agree that La Boétie died from an intestinal illness (stomach cramps and diarrhea), and he may have fallen victim to one of the recurring plagues that ravaged southwest France

---

20. For the quotations in this paragraph, see Frame, *Montaigne*, p. 54.

21. Although this letter was not published until the final item in the 1570 edition of La B's works, which M supervised, it is generally agreed that he began it in August 1563 (his father died in 1568). Because it predates the *Essays*, it is one of the earliest examples we have of M's literary ability.

during the sixteenth century.[22] (Bordeaux saw an outbreak of plague in July of 1563 and early in August *Parlement* was forced to shut down for over a week.) Before beginning a lengthy, minute account of La Boétie's last few days, Montaigne's letter details the personal reasons for the significance of his "last words":

> There is no doubt that if any man ought to render a good account of them, it is I, to a certain degree because throughout his illness he was as willing to talk to me as to anyone else and also because, due to the unique and brotherly friendship we had borne one another, I was fully aware of what he had intended, concluded, and willed during his lifetime—unquestionably as fully as any man could have of another. And because I knew these to be lofty, virtuous, and very sure resolutions—and, in short, admirable, I readily foresaw that if illness left him the means to be able to express himself, nothing would slip from him in such a necessity that was not great and replete with good example.

But the public nature of the letter, however, indicates that Montaigne also justified his meticulous account (it is more than ten pages long in the French edition) because of those virtuous characteristics of La Boétie that he saw as worthy of emulation (and public attention).

Montaigne Limns La Boétie's Portrait

By taking these opportunities to flesh out specific components of La Boétie's character—by lengthening his literary shadow on his friend—Montaigne gradually completes La Boétie's emerging portrait, revealing a figure whose traits serve as a pattern for him and, by extension, for us as well. Before turning to the *Essays*, where the commentary is extensive, we might note La Boétie's importance to Montaigne in the memorial to him,

---

22. M believed he was exposed to the plague in the Périgord region or the Agenais, "where he had been recently, 'and where he had left everyone infected'"; Paul Bonnefon, *Oeuvres complètes d'Estienne de La Boétie* (Bordeaux: G. Gounouilhou; Paris: J. Rouam, 1892), p. xxxiv.

appropriately phrased in Latin that was inscribed in the tower study where the *Essays* were written:

> Sadly deprived of Étienne de la Boétie, the sweetest, dearest, most intimate friend, the best, most learned, most perfect friend our age has seen, Michel de Montaigne, wishing to have some suitable memorial of their mutual love, of his gratitude, and of his fidelity, and finally able to realize it in these distinguished, learned furnishings, has dedicated his delight in study to him.[23]

How apt that the "delight in study" should be so dedicated to his friend in Montaigne's "study." Many of the books in his library were a legacy from La Boétie; so dedicating his "delight in study" to him is a profound acknowledgment of the degree to which he is imbued with La Boétie's example.

More than books for his library, of course, La Boétie's real legacy to Montaigne was the ability to look objectively at custom and received opinion and, when appropriate, to reject it responsibly—in short, the argument presented in the *Discourse on Voluntary Servitude*. It took years for Montaigne to incorporate the contents of this little volume into his life and work, but it is an essential theme of the *Essays*, which arguably represents Montaigne's response to his friend's legacy. Through them he communicates to his dead friend or, as in Conrad, his "secret sharer," by testing—via his understanding of the word *essay*—his ideas, by trying them out, by presenting them first to La Boétie and later to his audience.[24] He writes in "Vanity," probably with La Boétie—and maybe even us—in mind:

> No pleasure has any savor for me without communication. Not even a racy thought comes to my mind without my being annoyed at having produced it alone without anyone to offer

---

23. The actual text is a bit shaky but this translation is based on the text given in Pléiade 1, pp. xvi–xvii.

24. The word *essay* and the way in which M used *essai* emphasize the word's derivation from the Latin *exagium*, in the sense of weighing, and *exigere*, literally "to drive out or away" (as in to put at a distance from oneself) and, by extension, to examine, test, try out, as in a trial.

it to. . . . It would be annoying to be even in heaven strolling among those great and divine celestial bodies without the company of a companion."[25]

The earliest extended discussion of La Boétie in the *Essays* begins with a reference to "a discourse that he entitled 'Voluntary Servitude,' but those who did not know this have since quite correctly renamed 'Against One.' He wrote it, while still very young, as an *essay* in praise of freedom, against tyrants. . . . Still, it is far from being the best he could do. For if at the more advanced age when I knew him he had come up with a plan like mine of putting his fancies into writing, we would see many rare things, which would bring us quite close to antiquity's distinction."[26] Montaigne often refers self-deprecatingly to his own writings as "fancies," or "fantasies." But the *Essays*, taken in their entirety, represent Montaigne's attempt to understand himself. So if Montaigne considered the *Discourse on Voluntary Servitude* to be, like his own efforts, an "essay," or attempt at self-knowledge (here undertaken by his "secret sharer"), then the *Discourse* can be seen as part of Montaigne's extended project of defining *que sçay-je*, "what do I know?"

In Montaigne's emotional and intellectual portrait there is also this plaintive allusion to La Boétie: "Writing letters . . . is a kind of work in which my friends hold that I have some ability." In a later revision, once he had even more time to mull over his thoughts about La Boétie, he inserted a significant addition: "I would have been all the more willing to adopt that form for publishing my fantasies, if I had had someone to talk to. I needed what I once had, a certain relationship to draw me out, sustain me, and raise me up. . . . [W]ith a strong friend to write to, I would have been more attentive and confident than I am now, when I consider the various tastes of the public. And if I am not deceiving myself, I would have

---

25. From "Vanity," III, 9; Pléiade 1, p. 965; Pléiade 2, pp. 1032–33; V-S, pp. 986–87. Perhaps such a "savor" of "communication" explains the bond the librettist Boito felt for the composer Verdi when he wrote of their collaborative friendship: "The voluntary servitude I consecrated to that just, most noble and truly great man is the act of my life that gives me most satisfaction"; Fausto Torrefranco, "Arrigo Boito," *Musical Quarterly* 6, no. 4 (October, 1920): 538, 540–41.

26. *Selected Essays*, ed. Atkinson and Sices, p. 73

been more successful."[27] Because there was no one to read his letters with empathy and understanding, Montaigne appears to have been forced to fall back on a second-best literary form, writing "fantasies" that take into account "the varied tastes of the public."

Another indication of the emotional leverage La Boétie had over Montaigne exists in his description of the origin of the *Essays*, his "stupid enterprise": "It is a melancholy humor, and therefore a humor quite opposed to my natural temperament, caused by the solitary dejection into which I had plunged myself several years ago, that first put into my head this pipe dream of trying my hand at writing."[28] This sentence may in fact suggest the "solitary dejection" attendant on La Boétie's death as a stimulus to the composition of the *Essays*, especially when read in conjunction with a passage later in the essay: "Three and four times happy he who can entrust his pitiful old age into a friendly hand . . . O my friend! . . . My sorrow for him consoles and does me honor. Is it not a pious and happy duty of my life to be forever celebrating his death? Is there any pleasure that is as good as this deprivation?"[29] Despite Montaigne's resolute inward gaze, the ambivalent emotions he indicates—a happy celebration of death, sorrow as an honor—suggest that his *Essays* may well be his way of reciprocating La Boétie's legacy: looking at customary practices with a cold eye.

One "customary" practice upon which Montaigne cast a "cold eye," thanks to La Boétie, was death itself. In the letter he wrote his father describing La Boétie's final days, he admits, "I

---

27. From "A Consideration of Cicero," I, 40 [39]; Pléiade 1, p. 246; Pléiade 2, p. 256; V-S, p. 252. Given the nature of the two men's friendship and geographic proximity, it is reasonable to assume that there once existed a body of letters between them, though no trace of it exists today.

28. "The Affection of Fathers for Their Children," II, 8; Pléiade 1, p. 364; Pléiade 2, p. 404; V-S, p. 385. M is following the Renaissance medical belief in humors when he states that his usual temperament is positive (elsewhere he sees himself as being of a "sanguine" disposition), but that an abundance of the black bile in the melancholic humor would lead to a state of depression—for some Renaissance writers, a state conducive to creativity.

29. This passage, found in the 1595 edition raises several textual issues because part of it was crossed out several times; whether M made the corrections is unclear.

told him that I had blushed for shame that my courage had failed me upon hearing what he, who was involved in this illness, had had the courage to tell me"—specifically, he recounts later, La Boétie assured Montaigne—"my brother, my friend"—that he "had been prepared" for death "for a very long time and knew the entire lesson by heart." Montaigne admits to his father, ruefully, "Until then I had thought that God did not give us any much advantage over human disasters and had difficulty believing what I sometimes read about it in the histories; but having experienced such a proof of it, I praised God that it had been from a person who so loved me and whom I loved so dearly; and that this would serve me as an example—to play this same part in my turn."[30] Earlier in this passage, Montaigne describes how La Boétie begged him "to show in action that the discussions we had had together while we were healthy were not stated solely in the mouth but engraved deeply in the heart and soul, so they might be carried out at the earliest opportunity—adding that this was the real object of our studies and of philosophy." This significant quotation illustrates how both men sought to live their lives.

La Boétie's approach to death led to such assertions in "Through Philosophy We Learn How to Die," as "Cicero says that philosophy is nothing other than preparing for death" and "Death is the goal of our career, it is, of necessity, what we are aiming for."[31] But toward the end of his career, upon further reflection about La Boétie's example as it had played out in his own life, Montaigne realized that although we experience dying we cannot experience death. So, he pleaded, "enjoy one's being in good faith" and renounce attempts to "learn how to die." In a contemplative mood, he laid the groundwork for this advice in "Experience": "Now especially, when I perceive [my time to be alive] to be for so short a time, I want to increase its weight; I want to halt the swiftness of its flight by the swiftness of my grasp, and by strength in its use to compensate for the hurriedness of its flow: the briefer my possession of life, the deeper and fuller I have to make it."[32] Early in his life, in the essay "Friendship," and late in his

---

30. Pléiade 1, p. 1353

31. *Selected Essays*, ed. Atkinson and Sices, pp. 11, 14.

32. *Selected Essays*, ed. Atkinson and Sices, pp. 283, 278.

life, in "Experience," Montaigne makes equally evident the resonance of La Boétie's example for him.

In asserting the validity and veracity of his *Essays* as a self-portrait, Montaigne shows how reluctant he is to entrust others with the task: "I leave nothing about myself to be sought after and guessed at. . . . I would be willing to return from the other world to correct anyone who portrayed me other than I was, even to do me honor." Clarifying whom he has in mind, he alludes to La Boétie's personal valence for him in an addition to this sentence, "I well know that I will not leave behind me any guarantor even approximating the affection and understanding he had for me, that I have had for him. And there is no one I would be fully willing to rely on for my portrait; he alone possessed my true image, and he took it away with him. That is why I—myself—interpret myself, with such care."[33] This passage is an evocative description of the friends' mental and emotional relationship. La Boétie represented a powerful force in Montaigne's life: the only person capable of objectively appraising the "true image" in all the "chapters" that the *Essays* comprise. But he was dead. He could be addressed—and to a great extent he was addressed— only in absentia.

So what might we take from these many allusions to the otherwise literally overshadowed La Boétie so far? Thanks to Montaigne's dedicatory memorial, we know a "delight in study" was common to both authors; perhaps modeling a "delight in study" could stimulate the intellectual life of twenty-first-century readers and writers as well. Furthermore, La Boétie as a "secret sharer" with whom ideas can be essayed represents a person who would be as valuable today as he was in the sixteenth century. (Who could possibly want "to be even in heaven strolling among those great and divine celestial bodies without the company of a companion"?) Finally, a friend's encouragement is always valuable, especially when he provides the courage, the impetus, to believe that "fancies" are worth publishing—and does so with the advice to cast a cold eye on custom. This advice is as valid now as it

---

33. "Vanity," III, 9; Pléiade 1, p. 961 and n. 3 on this passage, pp. 1652–53; Pléiade 2, p. 1029 and n. "a," p. 1796; V-S, p. 983, n. 4. On this passage, see the discussion in Jean Starobinski, *Montaigne in Motion*, pp. 37–39; for some particularly trenchant remarks in Starobinski about La B's relation to M, see pp. 37–66.

was then and need not be restricted to ideas about death. No wonder we are beginning to see more clearly the portrait of someone who is a "guarantor," to be relied on fully to re-create a faithful representation. Who could not want a person who could be trusted to reproduce a "true image," obviating the need "to return from the other world to correct" a flawed portrait?

The *Discourse on Voluntary Servitude:* A Portrait without a Frame

La Boétie's major work, the *Discourse on Voluntary Servitude,* makes from Montaigne's sketch the complete portrait this profound thinker deserves. Yet its impact in the sixteenth century was likely even more multihued than its impact today, which in turn must inform our sense of its author. We must first decide exactly *what* it is, which requires an ear for La Boétie's prose. He is not a stylist in the same vein as Montaigne, who is never hortatory, or inflammatory. But La Boétie fulfills Montaigne's preference for vigorous prose that is "not legalistic, but rather soldierly." Biblical cadences often color his questions and pleas.[34] La Boétie's passion inspired the publishing of various excerpts from the *Discourse* during his lifetime, but they were then taken out of context to serve causes he would not have supported. Its vigor tempts the modern reader to quote extensively to convey its texture. Yet any attempt at a neutral description of it is merely a first step in trying to get at what it is—to say nothing about what has been made of it since La Boétie wrote it.

---

34. These cadences suggest a positive valence to the phrase—concept, even—of "voluntary servitude." Although it obviously is not one consonant with La B's purpose, there remains the idea that a person, for spiritual or emotional reasons, can serve willingly. For example Pausanias in Plato, *Symposium,* 184c refers to "willing subjugation" in the context of a lover serving the beloved in any way possible to communicate wisdom and virtue; see Alexander Nehamas and Paul Woodruff's edition of the *Symposium* (Indianapolis: Hackett Publishing Company, 1989, p. 18). Furthermore, the Douay version of St. Paul's epistle in 1 Corinthians 9:19 reads: "whereas I was free as to all, I made myself the servant of all, that I might gain more persons." Willingly serving God, the beloved, or a friend is not akin to La B's "voluntary servitude" but it is another way to construe the concept.

The warmth of his ardor animates his effort to understand a profound enigma: why do human beings consent to hand their natural-born, innate freedom over to powerful political leaders—tyrants, dictators? La Boétie defines his own struggle to understand in terms of the conflict between the rational and the irrational, the reasonable and the unreasonable. With a possible glance at Lucan, *De bello civili* (*Pharsalia*), he states his basic conundrum early: how does it happen "that so many men, so many towns, so many cities, so many nations at times tolerate a single tyrant who has no other power than what they grant him, who has no other power to harm them than inasmuch as they are willing to tolerate it, who could do ill to them only insofar as they would rather suffer it than oppose him."[35] More troubling still, this servitude arises not from "cowardice" but from the consent of the governed—ordinary people—and their "disdain or scorn" to confront the issue.

To save themselves, men must realize that "this lone tyrant does not have to be fought, there is no need to defeat him: he is defeated by himself if the country does not accept its servitude. Nothing must be taken from him; but he must be given nothing." Perhaps La Boétie is standing on its head Machiavelli's insight—that a ruler's power depends on coercing the people to accept his rule. The *Discourse* then argues that if the people refuse to acknowledge their ruler's power, that power would revert to them. Consequently, with a call that sounds to some like the advocacy of civil disobedience, La Boétie promises that people need only "resolve no longer to be slaves and you will be free!" With a nod to Plutarch, he conjures up an appropriate image: "I do not want you to push him or overthrow him, but merely no longer to sustain him and, like a great colossus whose base has

---

35. See p. 2. Might these words be echoed in the Declaration of Independence: "to assume among the powers of the earth, the separate and equal station to which the laws of nature and of nature's God entitle them. . . . That whenever any form of government becomes destructive to these ends, it is the right of the people to alter or to abolish it, and to institute new government, laying its foundation on such principles and organizing its powers in such form, as to them shall seem most likely to effect their safety and happiness."

been pulled away, you will see him collapse of his own weight and break up."[36]

But cowardice always hinders the necessary resolve. This "unfortunate vice" is "so deeply rooted" that La Boétie, using imagery drawn from Cicero, appeals to Nature and asserts a natural law, or right, to freedom: "If we lived with the rights that Nature has granted us and teachings she imparts, we would be naturally obedient to our parents, subject to reason, and slaves to no one. . . . [T]here is in our soul some natural seed of reason that, if fostered by good counsel and custom, flowers into virtue and on the other hand often is stifled and dies out because it cannot endure against vices that arise." He asserts that "liberty is natural, and by the same token, in my opinion . . . we are born not only in possession of our freedom but with the desire to defend it." Consequently, he is baffled by what he sees: "since this good mother [Nature] . . . has given us all the great gift of speech and words . . . what misfortune can so have denatured man, the only one truly born to live in freedom, and made him lose the memory of his original being, and the desire to regain it?"

To solve this puzzle he isolates three kinds of tyrants. First, there are those who "hold royal power through election by the people" because "the first reason for voluntary servitude is custom." Human beings have grown so accustomed to subjection "because men born under the yoke, and then raised and nurtured in serfdom, are content to live as they were born, without looking any farther; not thinking they have any other possessions or rights than what they have found, they take the state of their birth for their nature." Second, there are those who retain their tyranny "by force of arms"; they "behave in such a way that they are indeed known to be (as they say) in conquered territory." But, given his sixteenth-century audience, he concentrates his fire on tyrants of the third type, those who have gained power through "family succession." They are "usually no better . . . and regard the people who are under them as their hereditary slaves." These subjects "since they were born and raised in the bosom of tyranny . . . suck the tyrant's nature with their milk." Given this dynastic potential, he makes no distinction

---

36. See p. 8.

between king and tyrant, or between a good king and a bad tyrant. In the end, of course, there is little practical difference among these three types: "although the means of coming to power may differ, still the way they exercise it is just about the same. Those elected treat [subjects] as if they had taken on bulls to tame; the conquerors treat them as their prey; the successors think to treat them as their natural slaves."

La Boétie's insight into the tyrant's means and methods is indeed grim. As "the source and secret of domination, the basis and foundation of tyranny" he describes a system that is the opposite of participatory democracy: participatory tyranny. "There have always been five or six who had the tyrant's ear, and have gotten there by themselves or else were called by him to be accomplices in his cruelties and companions in his pleasures, to pander to his lusts and share in the goods he pillages." Accomplices, however, tend to multiply geometrically. "These six have six hundred who profit under them and they do with their six hundred what the six do to the tyrant. . . . Great is the following that comes after that; if anyone should wish to untangle this thread, he will see that not six thousand, but a hundred thousand, millions are linked to the tyrant by this cord." Meanwhile the tyrant, as La Boétie knows from reading Xenophon's dialogue *Hiero*, lives in perpetual fear nevertheless: he "never thinks that his power is secure until he has reached the point where he has no man of worth under him." In an insight suggestive of Elias Canetti's description of the "paranoid despot," La Boétie generalizes that tyrants "since they harm everyone . . . are obliged to fear everyone."[37]

Nevertheless, there must be some among all of the "natural slaves" living in this complicated web of tyranny who are "better born than the others, who feel the weight of the yoke and cannot help shaking it, who never grow used to subjection." In contrast to his ever-present contempt for those who have grown "weak and unmanly," he calls on "bold men [who] do not fear danger to get what they

---

37. Fear results in this more recent definition: "Als den paranoichen Typus des Machthabers könte man den bezeichnen, der sich die Gefahr mit allen Mitteln vom Leibe hält," Elias Canetti, *Masse und Macht* (Munich: Carl Hanser Verlag, 1960), p. 273; "The paranoiac type of ruler may be defined as one who uses every means to keep danger away from his person," *Crowds and Power*, trans. Carol Stewart (New York: Viking Press, 1962), p. 271.

demand, sensible men [who] do not avoid effort." They are what some might, with a jaundiced view, think of as aristocrats; more sympathetically, they are the "engaged" intellectual class, people who "cannot help looking to their natural privileges and recalling their predecessors and their original state . . . having clear understanding and a perceptive mind." Unlike "the ordinary people," members of this vital group "are not content . . . just to look immediately before their feet if they do not see what is ahead and behind. . . . They are men whose heads are well made to start with, who have refined them by study and learning. These men, even if liberty were completely lost and absent from the world, would imagine it and feel it in their minds and still savor it; servitude is not to their taste, no matter how it is dressed up." Because they are endowed with the ability to say no to the powerful, in other words, they possess the potential to be leaders of those not so endowed. La Boétie judges this to be a significant potential contribution because, again, "the source and secret of domination, the basis and foundation of tyranny" are rooted not merely in the people's acquiescence to it but also in the strategic organization of those supporting it.[38]

He illustrates his point with a folksy image borrowed from Erasmus: "To split wood [you use] wedges of the wood itself." Then he sets the scene: "The plowman and the artisan, though they may be enslaved, need not do any more than what they are told." But near the tyrant there are others "cadging and begging his favor. Not only must they do what he says, but also think of what he wants. . . . [T]hey have to break their backs, torture themselves, work themselves to death on his business . . . force their character, shed their own nature [and] be attentive to his words, his voice, his gestures, and his eyes; they should only have eyes, feet, and hands to look out for his wishes and to discover his thoughts." Fervently La Boétie demands: "Is this living happily? Is this what you call living? Is there anything in the world less bearable than this? . . . What condition is more miserable than living this way, not having anything for oneself, owing one's well-being, liberty, body, and life to someone else?"

---

38. Another passage from the Declaration of Independence lists a grievance against King George III: "He has made judges dependent on his will alone, for the tenure of their offices, and the amount and payment of their salaries."

Before launching into his peroration, La Boétie looks at those "wedges" to split wood—defined yet another way as people who "want to serve in order to have possessions"—in the light of friendship and its absence. He declares that history is full of people "who, after gaining the ear of princes by wicked means, either making use of their wickedness or exploiting their naïveté, were destroyed in the end by those very men"; in addition, "a tyrant never either is loved or himself loves" (more evidence for "the paranoiac type" of ruler). He predicates these assertions on a conviction dear to him—and to Montaigne—that "friendship is a sacred name, it is a holy thing: it never exists save between morally upright people and stems only from mutual esteem. It is sustained not so much by favors rendered as by proper living." Consequently, it is "hard to find assured love in a tyrant. For since he is above everyone else and has no companion, he is already beyond the limits of friendship, whose fair game is equality."

The peroration, when it arrives, is brief and vehement. "So once and for all, let us learn to do good." He then concludes: "I do think and I am not mistaken—since there is nothing so contrary to a generous, kindly God as tyranny—that He reserves a place down there for some special punishment of tyrants and their accomplices." He echoes the concluding speech of Xenophon's spokesman Ischomachus in the dialogue that, as we saw earlier, La Boétie had once translated entitled *The Oeconomicus: A Discussion on Estate Management*.[39] In it, Ischomachus insists that the gods give "despotic rule over unwilling subjects to those whom they judge worthy to live the life of Tantalus, of whom it is said that in hell he spends eternity, dreading a second death." La Boétie thus closes his *Discourse* by broadening its scope: to run a household, to manage an estate, or, particularly, to administer a state, implies choices with ethical, theological, and political consequences. Whatever the scale, it must be done well, and it must be for the common weal.

---

39. M was involved in the 1571 publication of this translation; he added chapter numbers and some of the marginal notes. O'Brien's essay in Tetel, *Étienne de La Boétie*, pp. 45–62, notes that La B was particularly adept at finding natural-sounding French expressions for Xenophon (p. 59).

The *Discourse on Voluntary Servitude* in Its Sixteenth-Century Frame

So much for a description the *Discourse on Voluntary Servitude* as it appears in the twenty-first century. What it says is clear; why he said it and how it has been read is not. So, to complement its present appearance we need to discover what it looked like in the sixteenth century. This is when the picture becomes cloudy. While what its earliest readers made of it adds another dimension to its description, there are many facets to their evidence. Montaigne, of course, was one of the first, yet he muddies our perspective; statements from other contemporaries rarely clarify it.

First of all, there is conflicting evidence about when the *Discourse* was in fact written. Toward the end of Montaigne's essay "Friendship" in the 1593 edition, he asks us to "listen a bit to this boy of sixteen."[40] Curiously, the 1580 and 1588 editions read "eighteen" instead of "sixteen"; the 1593 date is a correction Montaigne made in the margin of an earlier edition. So it would seem as if Montaigne sought to underscore the text's youthful origins. Moreover, at the beginning of the essay, he had already pointed out that La Boétie wrote it "while still very young as an essay in praise of freedom, against tyrants." Were we to listen to him, we would conclude that the *Discourse on Voluntary Servitude* was written either in 1546 or 1548. Another contemporary, the historian—particularly of the Wars of Religion—and later First President of the Paris *Parlement*, Jacques-Auguste de Thou (1553–1617), claimed La Boétie was nineteen when he wrote it.[41] (The motive for this assertion will be examined later.) If this is true, he was still a law student in Orléans, since he left for Bordeaux in 1553.

---

40. The quotations from M in the next several paragraphs, unless otherwise noted, are from "Friendship," I, 28 [27], *Selected Essays*, ed. Atkinson and Sices, pp. 73–86.

41. De Thou had high praise for La B, someone with "an admirable mind, a vast and profound erudition, and a marvelous facility for talking and writing; capable of great things, if he had been closer to Court and if his premature death had not prevented the public from reaping the fruits of so sublime a genius"; *Historiarum sui temporis tomus secundus* (Paris: Ambroise et Jérome Drouart, 1606), p. 219 ff.

Moreover, these early dates do not help clear up what appear to be allusions in the *Discourse* to historical and literary matters that arose later than the years 1546 to 1549. For example, they neglect the implications of Guillaume de Lur-Longa, the man La Boétie replaced in the Bordeaux *Parlement*. When La Boétie addresses him ("in writing to you, Longa"), he was in Paris serving in its *Parlement*. If we can assume he wrote Lur-Longa while Lur-Longa (who died in 1556) was alive, that expands the *terminus ad quem*, the date when he could last have worked on the *Discourse* from 1548 to 1556. Lur-Longa's name also comes up in the context of apparent references to the preamble of the *Édit de Fontainebleau* of January 1552 and the *Édit du semestre* of April 1554.[42] Neither reference, though, helps to specify a composition or publication date.

A reference La Boétie makes to the Pléiade also presents a problem regarding the *Discourse*'s date. Because its manifesto, Du Bellay's *Défense et illustration de la langue française*, was published in 1549, it is a bit premature for La Boétie to praise at the very same time "our French poetry—now not merely refurbished but, it seems, made completely new by our Ronsard, our Baïf, our du Bellay." As for Ronsard ("those fine tales . . . which I seem to see the talent of our Ronsard enjoying [with such pleasure!] so ably in his *Franciade*"), an interesting literary fact occurred in January 1554 when La Boétie's brother-in-law, Lancelot de Carle, promised King Henri II that his reign would be glorified in Ronsard's forthcoming poem *Franciade*. This is the first public announcement of Ronsard's plan and the king urged its publication; however, four of the books (out of a projected twenty-four) were not published until 1572. The best conclusion we might draw from this inconclusive evidence is that there may have been several manuscripts of the *Discourse on Voluntary Servitude* available,

---

42. Both edicts tried to reform the judicial system in the king's favor thereby increasing his revenue. For the second edict, see Guy Demerson, "Les *exempla* dans le *Discours de la servitude*: une rhétorique datée," in Tetel, *Étienne de La Boétie*, pp. 195–224. For the *Édit du semestre*, see Michel Magnien, "Sur Un Échange Poétique Méconnu Entre Dorat et La Boétie Autour de l' *Édit du semestre* (1554), *Jean Dorat: poète humaniste de la Renaissance*, ed. Christine de Buzon and Jean-Eudes Girot, Actes du Colloque International, Limoges, June 6–8, 2001, Travaux d'Humanisme et Renaissance, no. 170 (Geneva: Librarie Droz, 2007), pp. 369–92.

but we cannot know when La Boétie drafted the first one, only that there may have been revisions to it. Furthermore, it must be asked: Was it La Boétie who made the revisions before he died in 1563 or was it someone else?

If we knew why sixteenth-century readers thought it was written, we might also gain a better perspective on its immediate impact. Jacques-Auguste de Thou, for example, dated the *Discourse*'s publication to 1549 because he believed that it was provoked by the salt-tax revolt (la révolte des Pitauds) in and around Bordeaux, which went on for more than ten days during August of 1548. French kings had usually refrained from exacting a tax on salt from this region but Henri II broke with tradition and imposed a tax, the *gabelle*, in 1548.[43] De Thou believed La Boétie was so horrified by the punishments executed over the course of three months by the avenging Constable Anne de Montmorency, leader of the ten thousand royal troops sent in to quell the situation in October, that he wrote the *Discourse* in protest.[44] Allusions to events post 1549 belie de Thou's assertion, however. Furthermore, none of the many historical examples La Boétie uses to bolster his argument occurs in the sixteenth century or in what would be his recent past.[45]

---

43. Salt was vitally important during the Renaissance to flavor and preserve food. Taxing it was an equally important source of royal revenue. Bordeaux, in a region *de grandes gabelles*, meant that it presented a huge temptation to royal coffers. See Knecht, *The Rise and Fall of Renaissance France*, pp. 21–23.

44. Knecht, *The Rise and Fall*, describes the situation: "Matters came to a head on 21 August [1548], when Tristan de Moneins [governor of Bordeaux] . . . was lynched as he was about to negotiate with local dignitaries. Twenty *gabeleurs* were killed at the same time and their bodies covered with salt as a gesture of derision" (p. 246). Montmorency did not arrive in Bordeaux until October; by the time he left on November 22nd, there had been 150 executions (Knecht, p. 247). Montaigne witnessed these events ("In my youth I saw a gentleman . . . hard pressed by a frenzied populace's agitation . . . he was killed cruelly." *Essays,* "Differing Outcomes of the Same Plan," I, 24 [23]). Did La B see any of these atrocities? We cannot be certain. Yet Montmorency's aftereffects were surely not short-lived.

45. No one takes seriously the anecdote poet and historian Agrippa d'Aubigné (1552–1630) told that the *Discourse* resulted from La B's anger at the court because a guard, irritated by La B's demands to enter a ballroom in the Louvre, dropped his halberd on La B's foot.

Finally, at the risk of Montaigne's literary shadow reappearing to obscure rather than reveal, we might turn to him for contemporary comment about the origin and meaning of the *Discourse*—though we know his information about when it was written is of little avail. In the last paragraph of "Friendship" we learn that La Boétie "dealt with this topic [voluntary servitude] in his youth just as an exercise, an ordinary topic that has been mistreated in thousands of places in books." By stressing that his essay was a commonplace topic for what he termed *une exercitation*, or "exercise," Montaigne reminded the Renaissance reader of the rhetorical tradition—known as *declamatio*, the practice of declamation—stretching from Erasmus' *De Copia* (1512) back to Cicero and his rhetorical handbook *De Inventione* and to the ancient Greek rhetorical schools of the third and second century BCE.

The tradition, which both he and La Boétie learned in school, showed students how to develop effective writing and speaking habits by analyzing and developing their ideas in an *exercitatio*, a rhetorical exercise displaying specific skills (for example, imitation, amplification, and variation). They would conclude their study with a presentation (*declamatio*) in which they would "declaim" a text that could be centered on an ethical concern, a concern that was deliberative in nature (*suasoria*, persuasive eloquence), or a forensic, judicial concern (*controversia*, a subject of debate). The latter was usually assigned to advanced students, as in debating societies today, because they had to be able both to attack and to defend a given proposition.

Clearly La Boétie was well versed in rhetorical principles, so perhaps his treatise is best read merely as a young demonstration of his rhetorical ability.[46] It could be argued that—like the *declamatio* of Erasmus' *In Praise of Folly* (written 1509; published 1511)— La Boétie would have expected his readers to understand that his text was imitating Erasmus' "heroine" and spokesperson, Stultitia (Folly herself), sending a signal similar to hers: do not assume,

---

46. See Jean Lafond, "Le *Discours de la servitude voluntaire* et la Rhétorique de la déclamation," *Mélanges sur la littérature de la Renaisssance. A la mémoire de V.-L. Saulnier*, preface by Pierre Georges Castex (Geneva: Droz, 1984), pp. 735–45, reprinted in Lafond, *Lire, vivre òu mènent les mots: aux formes brèves de la prose*, (Paris: Champion, 1999), pp. 33–45. Lafond argues that La B did not believe in the conclusions his rhetoric would have prescribed.

reader, that this text represents my true beliefs. Early in his treatise, La Boétie even draws attention to his argument's hypothetical basis: "Let us therefore seek to *guess, if we can* how this stubborn willingness to serve has thus become so deeply rooted thus, that it now seems the very love of liberty is not so natural" (emphasis added).[47]

Here Montaigne's shadow helps us to understand a rhetorical tradition that would have been familiar to La Boétie but less so to us. Yet La Boétie, as does any author, uses rhetoric in the *Discourse on Voluntary Servitude* to convey meaning. For Montaigne, this meaning raised a red flag—so much so that he decided not to make it more available to sixteenth-century readers. But before examining why this could be so, we might examine the clue provided by an interchange between Montaigne and Henri de Mesmes, a French humanist who became a member of Charles IX's Privy Council. The definitive Smith-Magnien text that we have used for this translation is based on a manuscript originally owned by de Mesmes, now one of four manuscripts in the Bibliothèque Nationale (fonds français, 839). Given his circle of intellectual friends, we might expect this nobleman to have made La Boétie's manuscript more available by circulating it within his coterie. But he did not. He instead grouped it with other treatises about which he had significant reservations: they contained "light and vain discourses by visionary dreamers who do not understand the State."[48]

Other contemporaries had their doubts about the *Discourse* as well. On April 30, 1570, Montaigne, for example, began his letter dedicating La Boétie's translation of Plutarch's "Rules of Marriage" to the same Henri de Mesmes as follows: "One of men's most notable follies is to use the power of their understanding to blast and destroy common, received opinions that bring us some satisfaction and

---

47. See Magnien's explanation of this position in the additional notes to the Smith-Magnien edition, pp. 90–92. Some modern commentators, taking a cue from Sainte-Beuve's comments in 1853 and 1854 (*Causeries du Lundi*), agree. They dismiss the *Discourse on Voluntary Servitude*, interpreting it as an impassioned oration, one that a modern-day Demosthenes might give to defend republican, revolutionary, or libertarian positions.

48. For this pronouncement, see de Mesmes, "Contre La Boétie," in *De la servitude volontaire*, ed. Gontarbert, p. 203; for de Mesmes' entire text, pp. 196–211.

contentment. . . . [I]n order to seem to have a bolder and more active mind . . . these people jangle their souls out of a peaceful and restful state of being so as to fill it eventually—after a long quest—with doubt, anxiety, and fever." Given what he considers Protestants' attempts "to blast and destroy" the common, received opinion that constituted the religious tenets of Catholicism, Montaigne sees a potential danger in enlarging the public for La Boétie's work by adding propaganda grist to the mills of the Huguenots.[49] These were not dangers the dead La Boétie had to face but they were problematic for some late-sixteenth-century readers.

When he had the opportunity and when it would have been appropriate, Montaigne nevertheless contended with these hazards by refusing to publish not only the *Discourse on Voluntary Servitude* but also the "Memoir Concerning the Edict of January 1562." This decision could be considered as another example of Montaigne being guilty of reinforcing La Boétie's shadowy existence. Yet his reasons are instructive, especially in conjunction with Henri de Mesmes' comment regarding the reception the *Discourse* received in the sixteenth century. Referring to the work at the end of the essay "Friendship," Montaigne notes that he "discovered that this work has since been brought to light, and to an evil end, by those who seek to upset and change the state of our government without caring whether they improve it." Because "they have tossed other writings into the mill—I have decided not to put it here"—that is, in the first edition of the *Essays* (1580).[50]

This is what had happened: sections of the *Discourse* had been published by Huguenots, angered at continued persecutions. These came to a head during August of 1572 with the Saint Bartholomew's Day massacre that initiated a series of targeted assassinations of

---

49. Thinking of the Bible, perhaps Matthew 18:3–4, M adds, "It is not without reason that childlike simplicity has been so commended by truth itself"; Pléiade 1, p. 1361.

50. For how a perfect friendship, as opposed to an ordinary one, can be realized only after one friend dies—coupled with a discussion of Hans Holbein's painting "The Ambassadors" (1533)—see Saul Frampton, *When I am Playing With My Cat, How Do I Know That She Is Not Playing With Me: Montaigne and Being In Touch With Life* (New York: Pantheon Press, 2011), pp. 32-40; 208–10.

Protestant leaders lasting over several weeks.[51] Although this strife was centered in Paris, emotions ran high and murderous recriminations spread throughout France. Put on the defensive and desperate to spur their partisans, Huguenots published a partial, mangled passage that appeared in 1574 (*Le Réveille-matin* ["alarm call"] *des François*)[52] and a complete text in 1577, republished in 1578 (*Mémoires de l'estat de France, sous Charles Neufiesme*).[53] Later in the sixteenth century, a number of Huguenots were not at all troubled by the treatise. They were the "fighters against monarchs," the Monarchomachs, who referred to the treatise to bolster their opposition to an absolute

---

51. For this significant period, see Knecht, *The Rise and Fall*, pp. 413–66. The Protestant leaders were present in Paris for the wedding of Henri de Navarre, the future king Henri IV, a Protestant, with the sister of the current king, Charles IX, both Catholics.

52. This version was a translation in French by Simon Goulart from a Latin text published in 1573, *Dialogi ab Eusebio Philadelpho cosmopoliti in Gallorum et caeterorum nationum gratiam compositi*. The full title of the 1574 edition is *Le Réveille-matin des François et de leurs voisins, composé par Eusebe Philadelphe Cosmopolite en forme de dialogues*. Using the pseudonym Eusebius (260–340 CE), the "author" aligns himself with someone who, though identified as an early ecclesiastical historian, challenged Church authority. Mitchiko Iagolnitzer has established that the "author" is really two men: François Hotman and Hugues Doneau; see *Bulletin de la Société de Montaigne*, 5th Series (April–September, 1976): 99–109. Hotman (*Franco-Gallia*; Latin, 1573; French, 1574) and Doneau were Protestants with legal training; the former was linked to the Monarchomachs; see Paul-Alexis Meillet, *Les Traités Monarchomaques: Confusion des Temps, Résistance Armée, et Monarchie Parfaite (1560–1600)*, Travaux d'Humanisme et Renaissance, no. 184 (Geneva: Libraire Droz, 2007).

53. The *Mémoires de l'estat de France, sous Charles Neufiesme*, complete with stories and documents recounting Catholic atrocities perpetrated on Huguenots, was widely distributed in France, though printed in Geneva. The version of the *Discourse* it contained, with the first use of the words "against one" (as it was rechristened by Protestants), is the basis for the text of the *Discourse* edited by Françoise Bayard (Paris: Imprimerie Nationale, 1992) because she believes it precedes the Henri de Mesmes manuscript, the one generally accepted as the standard text. Remember, too, M did not include the "Memoir" in the 1570 edition of La B's works because he did not want, even then, to abandon it "to the coarse and heavy air of so unpleasant a season."

monarch, even to the (theoretical) extent of tyrannicide. The publication in 1579 of *Vindiciae contra tyrannos* ("Defenses Against Tyrants")
could well have been another factor influencing Montaigne's
decision to keep La Boétie's *Discourse* out of the first edition of
his *Essays* in 1580 because of the similarities between this tract
and La Boétie's. Many assign its authorship to Philippe de Mornay (Du
Pleissis-Mornay), one of the Monarchomachs, who was a Huguenot
philosopher and adviser to Henri de Navarre, who would later become
king Henri IV.[54]

Consequently, since the *Discourse* was obviously circulating in manuscript and in truncated publications, Montaigne grew protective of
his deceased friend because, as he says at the end of "Friendship,":
"There never was a better citizen, or one devoted to his country's
peace, or a greater enemy to the disturbances and revolutions of
his time. He would much rather have used his abilities to suppress
them than to furnish them with the wherewithal to arouse them
further. His mind was patterned after other ages than this."[55] A less
charitable interpretation of Montaigne's decision not to include the
Discourse as the centerpiece of the first book of *Essays* might conclude
that Montaigne wanted to save his own skin. In the last paragraph of
"Friendship" he says he omits the *Discourse* "so that the author's memory not be tarnished." Perhaps Montaigne feared that it was his own
reputation that would be "tarnished" by including it among his own
works. At any rate, Montaigne was not above backhandedly criticizing
his contemporaries for their treatment of La Boétie.

The theme common to both Montaigne's and de Mesmes' anxiety about the latent dangers of the *Discourse* is what it advocates
rejecting. Neither man is comfortable with saying no to authority,
be it that of the state or the church. The church, however, is para-
mount among their concerns with regard to the *Discourse* because the
Huguenots had already insisted on highlighting what they read as its
challenges to Catholicism. But there is one more sixteenth-century

---

54. De Mornay lived from 1549 until 1623; in the 1580s he developed a
friendship with Montaigne. The *Vindiciae contra tyrannos* was signed "Junius
Brutus," which could refer to Lucilius Junius Brutus, who rose up against
the Tarquins or Marcus Junius Brutus, one of the conspirators against Julius
Caesar. The double reference was no doubt intentional.

55. *Selected Essays*, ed. Atkinson and Sices, p. 86.

reader who seizes on the *Discourse*'s powerful call for republican reforms. His obscurity does not hide the fact that he is the first in a long line of interpreters—stretching to the present day—who perceive its power to throw a monkey wrench into those structures of power in an ostensibly democratic state that run counter to the freedom of the individual. Jacopo Corbinelli, an anti-Medicean republican, was a Florentine exile living in Paris. On November 4, 1570, he wrote a friend of his in Padua, Vincenzo Pinelli, as follows: "I would like to have a copy of a writing that I have seen in the most elegant French, 'on voluntary servitude,' which Brutus himself could not have said better. I read it; it is something learned and recondite but for these times dangerous."[56] Although Corbinelli's motives may be ambiguous, his evocation of Brutus puts him in squarely in the camp of those opposing oppression in favor of individual freedom (and welcoming a compatriot in the La Boétie whom he met in the *Discourse*).

The *Discourse on Voluntary Servitude*'s Portrait as Seen through Several Eyes

In light of this discussion of the *Discourse on Voluntary Servitude*'s sixteenth-century reception, we now seek the final dimension of La Boétie's literary portrait: what his treatise has meant to those who have read it in the decades, and then centuries, after his death. This reception only begins with Montaigne's desire to protect his friend's memory; by 1580, as we have seen, when the *Essays* were first published, La Boétie's work had already proven its disruptive potential. The privilege allowing Montaigne to publish the first edition of his *Essays* was dated in Bordeaux on May 9, 1579. Two days earlier, the Bordeaux *Parlement* had ordered the public burning of a book containing, among other things, the first complete edition of the *Discourse*

---

56. For the French and Italian text, see Panichi, *Plutarchus redivivus?*, p. 23. Again, the double reference to Junius Brutus, as in the signing of *Vindiciae contra tyrannos*, was probably intentional. Panichi notes that Corbinelli had Catherine de' Medici as a patron, and that, curiously enough, M was in Paris that November overseeing his publication of La B's works.

on Voluntary Servitude.[57] Montaigne apparently saw himself ultimately as defending his friend's memory from the potential distortions of mean-spirited Protestants. Safeguarding La Boétie's reputation may even have led Montaigne to de-emphasize the treatise's scholarly, intellectual thrust. Never does he use the word *discours* to refer to it, though he never ceased to admire La Boétie's agile challenges to received ideas and opinions—his ability, in short, to think outside the box, as the *Discourse* in question so ably demonstrated.

Comments from Montaigne and his contemporaries, inconclusive as they are, leave ample room for more recent readers to offer their own opinions about how the rhetoric of the *Discourse on Voluntary Servitude* informs its meaning. Richard Regosin, for example, stresses the contradictory character of a text "that aims both at theory and practice, that both reinforces and undermines the one because it also seeks to be the other."[58] His careful literary analysis of this "monstrous" text (monstrous in its "divergent form and scandalous reasoning") comprises an excellent, sympathetic demonstration of La Boétie's "perplexity," and hence the challenge facing anyone who tries to write successfully about both freedom and politics. And Nadia Gontarbert, who offers what she terms a "polyphonic" reading and a "political one," calls for a "reappropriation" of how La Boétie works with language.[59]

---

57. This was the third volume of the second edition of *Mémoires de l'estat de France, sous Charles Neufiesme.* The burning occurred on the Place de l'Ombrière, directly in front of the building where the *Parlement* met. See Floyd Gray, "Montaigne et le Tombeau de La Boétie," in Tetel, *Étienne de La Boétie*, p. 268. However, in Reims in 1577 Odet de La Noue had published *Description de la Tyrannie, et des Tyrans, avec les moyens de se garantir de leur joug* ("Description of Tyranny, Tyrants, With the Means to Protect Oneself Against Their Yoke"). It was a complete version of the *Discourse*, but not attributed to La B. (In a brief study, published in 1919, Guy de Pourtalès identified Odet de La Noue as a late-sixteenth-century "poet and Huguenot soldier.")

58. "'Mais O Bon Dieu, Que Peut Estre Cela?' La Boétie's *La Servitude Volontaire* and the Rhetoric of Political Perplexity," in Tetel, *Étienne de La Boétie*, p. 260.

59. For her two readings, see her edition *De la servitude volontaire ou Contr'un*, pp. 131–90; for her language analysis, "La Servitude Volontaire: Pour Une

The *Discourse*'s potential began to be recognized long before the late twentieth century, of course. Though it lay dormant until the eighteenth century, a Protestant publisher in The Hague added it to a five-volume publication of Montaigne in 1727 giving the author as La Boétie—the first edition since the *Essays* had been put on the Roman Catholic Church's *Index of Prohibited Books* in 1676. La Boétie also appeared in abbreviated versions reprinted during the French Revolution (in 1789 and 1790). In nineteenth-century France, several editions were published in connection with specific religious and political stances: Abbé Frédéric de Lamennais, a fervent advocate of religious freedom, brought out an edition in 1835, and there were five more French editions in the nineteenth century before Paul Bonnefon did in 1892 what Montaigne had refused to do: publish La Boétie's complete works.

But the *Discourse* also drew attention outside of France. In the United States, Henry David Thoreau was aware of it in 1849 when he wrote "Resistance to Civil Government"—better known as "On Civil Disobedience"—and Emerson wrote of La Boétie's "world-warming spark / which dazzles me in midnight dark."[60] Leo Tolstoy's reading of both La Boétie and Thoreau had repercussions not only for his own life but also for Mahatma Gandhi's; Tolstoy's analysis of governmental power in fact mirrors La Boétie: "The power of the government rests on public opinion, and possessing power they can always support the sort of public opinion they require by their whole organization, officials, law courts, schools, the Church, even the Press. Public opinion produces the power, power produces public opinion; and it seems as if there were no escape from this position."[61] Tolstoy's rejection of tyranny also reflects an

---

Réappopriation du Langage," in Tetel, *Étienne de La Boétie*, pp. 307–16. For more on language, see in the same collection Jamil Chaker, "*Sémiotique des valeurs dans le* Contr'un," pp. 349–62.

60. Ralph Waldo Emerson, *Collected Poems and Translations*, ed. Harold Bloom and Paul Kane (New York: Penguin, 1994 [The Library of America]), p. 66.

61. "Patriotism and Christianity" (March 29, 1894), in Leo Tolstoy, *The Works: The Kingdom of God and Peace Essays*, vol. 20, trans. Aylmer Maude (London: Oxford University Press, 1935), Centenary Edition for the Tolstoy Society, section 16, p. 562. Based on Luke 17:21, Tolstoy's *The Kingdom*

awareness of La Boétie: "The misery of nations is caused not by particular persons but by the particular order of society under which the
people are so tied up together that they find themselves all in the power
of a few men, or more often of one single man: a man so perverted by
his unnatural position as arbiter of the fate and lives of millions, that
he is always in an unhealthy state, and always suffers more or less from
a mania of self-aggrandizement, which only his exceptional position
conceals from general notice."[62] And Tolstoy inserted a lengthy quotation from the *Discourse on Voluntary Servitude* in *The Law of Love and
the Law of Violence*, written as he was dying.[63]

Two years earlier Tolstoy, again in language reminiscent of La Boétie,
reminded Gandhi that "the oppression of a majority by a minority,
and the demoralization inevitably resulting from it, is a phenomenon
that has always occupied me and has done so most particularly of
late." Furthermore, he suggested that Gandhi should remember not
only that "those who enjoy power propagate these new sophistries and
support them so skillfully that they seem irrefutable, even to many of
those who suffer the oppression these theories seek to justify" but also
that "the scientific justifications of the principle of coercion . . . are not
merely weak but absolutely invalid, yet they are so much needed by those
who occupy privileged positions that they believe in them . . . blindly."[64]

---

of God Is Within You took these ideas even further. It was fundamental to
Gandhi's intellectual development and remains influential for today's
Christian anarchism.

62. "Thou Shalt Not Kill," (August 8, old style, 1900) in Leo Tolstoy,
Recollections and Essays, vol. 21, trans. Aylmer Maude (Oxford University
Press, for the Tolstoy Society; London: Humphrey Milford, 1937), p. 198.

63. *The Law of Love and the Law of Violence*, trans. Mary Koutouzow Tolstoy
(New York: Rudolph Field, 1948), pp. 42–45; see pp. 30–32 of this volume.
For the original, see Leo Tolstoy, *La Loi de l'amour et la loi de la violence* (Paris:
Dorbon-aîné, 1910), chap. 8, pp. 101–5.

64. From "A Letter to a Hindu," written from Yasnaya Polyana, December
14, 1908, in *Mahatma Gandhi and Leo Tolstoy Letters*, ed. B. Srinivasa Murthy
(Long Beach, CA: Long Beach Publications, 1987), pt. 1, p. 44; pt. 4, pp. 51,
53. (The year 1908 was also the year Gandhi translated John Ruskin's 1862
collection of articles, *Unto This Last*, into Gujarati and called it *Sarvodya*,
meaning "the well-being or progress of all"—a phrase Gandhi used to describe
the universal uplift he hope his political philosophy would achieve.) Dr.

As we shall see, these considerations will reverberate through Gandhi to Philip Glass.

Thoreau, Tolstoy, and Gandhi constitute a powerful reception history that influenced twentieth-century interpretations of the *Discourse*. Thoreau is linked to Tolstoy and Gandhi because, like them, he advocated nonviolent resistance to and nonviolent cooperation with oppressive regimes. Tolstoy stands apart, though, because his interpretation of La Boétie is rooted in his almost fanatical devotion to Christianity, which he orchestrated with neo-socialist overtones. In the latter half of the century, Harry Kurz read the *Discourse* as an antitotalitarian essay; for example, when he "rendered" it into English in 1942, he emphasized its overt challenge to Hitler by the title he gave it: *Anti-Dictator: The* Discours sur la servitude volontaire *of Étienne de la Boétie.*[65] More recently libertarians have found much to admire in it. For example, Murray Newton Rothbard brought out *The Politics of Obedience: The Discourse of Voluntary Servitude* in 1975, and revised it in 1997, because he linked La Boétie to his own ideas about human rights and their vulnerability to the state.

Conclusion

We have now brought La Boétie out of the shadows—Montaigne's, of course, as well as those of the intervening centuries. The easel now holds La Boétie's completed portrait. Sometimes portraits do more than merely freeze their subjects in time. Often they suggest attributes, characteristics that the painter believes viewers should pause over, even admire. At this point Montaigne ought to be no more than a barely visible trace in the portrait. La Boétie, in full view, has turned the table, removed himself from his friend's shadow, and stands before us a model. We might conclude by citing a Latin

---

Martin Luther King Jr. was indebted to both Tolstoy and Gandhi for his ideas about religion and social justice.

65. According to Hitler's *Mein Kampf*, "A clever conqueror will . . . impose his demands on the conquered by installments. For a people that makes a voluntary surrender saps its own character. . . . The more such exhortations are suffered without resistance" the harder it is to oppose them; for the full citation, see *The New York Review of Books*, 59:10 (June 7, 2012), p. 36, n. 4.

poem that La Boétie, exemplifying honesty and integrity through the voice of the poem, dedicated to Montaigne. Here, of course, La Boétie is in the driver's seat, observing that the two of them are bound together "by natural instinct and a love of virtue, which is the greatest charm of friendship." But suddenly the poem shifts in intensity. There is a veiled critique, rather like that of an older brother chastening a younger one:

> once your virtue is matured and strengthened by age,
> Then—and my love does not blind me—you will be able to vie
> with the greatest.[66]

This was during a period in his life when a modern critic referred to Montaigne, then in his late twenties, as "the young hedonist."[67]

---

66. At the end of the first of two volumes of La B's works, including his translations of Xenophon and Plutarch, which M published in 1571, there were twenty-eight Latin poems, *Poemata*. The third, "*Ad Michaelem Montanum*," was 322 lines in hexameter that, in "Friendship," M calls an "excellent satire in Latin." He reminded his readers thereby of a genre perfected by Roman writers that pointed out human failings, usually with ridicule and heavy irony, so individuals or society as a whole would mend their ways. The context of the lines in question are: *Te, Montane, midi cases socialite in omens / et natural patens et amorist grater illex / virtus . . . Affligunt ita me leviora beantque/ad summa indocilem, tantum mediocribus aptum. / At tibi certamen maius, quem scimus amici/nobilibus vitiis habilem et virtutibus aeque. / Sed tu iam haud dubie meliora capessis eoque/miror victorem laetor quoque. . . . At virtus cum se firmaverit aevo, / tum poteris (nec fallit amor) contendere summis; / tam bona perraro ingeniis sors contigit altis.* "You, Montaigne, have been bound to me once and for all by natural instinct and a love of virtue, which is the greatest charm of friendship. . . . I am incapable of the greatest things, and am suited only for the mediocre. But as for you, you are engaged in a loftier struggle. Your friends know that your errors as well as your strengths spring from greatness. . . . But once your virtue is matured and strengthened by age, then—and my love does not blind me—you will be able to view with the greatest"(lines 23–25; 35–38; 41–43). See Robert D. Cottrell, "An Introduction to La Boétie's Three Latin Poems Dedicated to Montaigne," *Montaigne Studies* 3, no. 1 (September, 1991): 26–29.

67. Referring to the decade from 1533 to 1563; Donald Frame, *Montaigne's Discovery of Man: The Humanization of a Humanist* (New York: Columbia University Press, 1955), pp. 11–29.

Although the immediate context for the remonstrance was his fear that Montaigne lacked self-discipline and risked impetuously flinging away his life on women and high living, La Boétie is here fulfilling what Montaigne defines as "one of the first duties of friendship": administering "cautions and corrections."[68] His frank judgment reads almost as if he were casting himself as a confessor, though one who has experienced similar temptations. The message is couched in a reference to the fable of "Hercules at the Crossroads" (line 132 ff.), which was often used in medieval and Renaissance literature to reinforce the choice of virtue over pleasure. He gently reminds his friend that, though he has been tempted (and will be tempted throughout his career), he must resist threats to his inherent virtue—a trait that La Boétie firmly believed Montaigne possessed. Even if the poem's voice is not La Boétie's as such, the poem's argument, taken as a whole, exhorts Montaigne to adhere unwaveringly to virtue's path. One commentator has suggested that La Boétie, while acknowledging the "hidden accord of nature" that linked them, "does not appear optimistic about the growth of the more important element of friendship, *virtus*. . . . He is doubtful about a teacher's success in molding the character of his student, in making him virtuous, something Montaigne seems to have asked him to do."[69] Even so, being able to say no to a friend is a distinctive trait, one that further informs his greatest work.

It frees La Boétie once and for all from any shadows whatsoever; it makes him a model worth imitating. It is what makes him worthy of the citizens of Sarlat-la-Canéda deciding in 1892 to erect a marble statue in his memory on the Place de la Rigaudie, facing the Palais de Justice.[70] Here La Boétie stands erect, proudly

---

68. In "Friendship," I, 28 [27], *Selected Essays*, ed. Atkinson and Sices, p. 75.

69. James S., Hirstein, "La Boétie's Neo-Latin Satire," *Montaigne Studies*, 3, 1 (September, 1991), p. 66.

70. The sculptor, Tony Nöel, made no effort to make La B look like anything other than a generic young man. (M paired him with Socrates in a discussion of "ugliness"—physical not spiritual—ugliness; "Physiognomy," III, 12, *Selected Essays*, ed. Atkinson and Sices, p. 221). He also left it to our imagination to determine what he was holding in his left hand. Local newspaper articles describing the occasion foreshadow the polarity in many subsequent interpretations of La B's significance: some hailed him as a political theorist

determined, with his right hand reaching out in an open, welcoming gesture; in his left hand, index finger marking his place, he clasps (it has to be) the *Discourse on Voluntary Servitude*'s manuscript. Its rhetoric and meaning have challenged readers for centuries, but its force could not be clearer. In his powerful summons to reject unwarranted authority, La Boétie is adamant: the people must protest when their government organizes structures of power to thwart individual freedom. As Philip Glass puts it in the final lines of his opera *Satyagraha*, based on episodes in Gandhi's life and composed in 1980: "When righteousness withers away and evil rules the land, we come into being, age after age, and take visible shape, and move, a man among men for the protection of good, thrusting back evil and setting virtue on her seat again."[71]

James B. Atkinson

---

who advocated freedom from tyranny while others, following M's lead, believed he loyally defended the Roman Catholic Church when reformists attacked its tenets.

71. For use of this sentence on a special occasion, see Alex Ross, "Number Nine," *The New Yorker*, February 13 and 20, 2012, p. 117.

A NOTE ON THE TEXT

This translation is based on Estienne de La Boétie, *De la Servitude Volontaire ou Contr'un*, edited by Malcolm Smith, with additional annotation and a bibliography by Michel Magnien (Geneva: Librarie Droz, 2001). Smith's first edition appeared in 1987. After his death in 1994, Magnien's revised edition, with more than twenty-five pages of additional material, appeared as part of the Droz "Textes Littréraires Français" series. The annotation of the two editors is indispensable.

Also Consulted

Étienne de La Boétie, *De la servitude volontaire, ou Contr'un*, ed. Nadia Gontarbert, Collection Tel (Paris: Gallimard, 2005). This edition also includes, with commentary, the useful "Contre La Boétie," pp. 196–211, by Henri de Mesmes, and La Boétie's *Mémoire touchant l'édit de janvier 1562*.

Étienne de La Boétie, *Discours de la servitude volontaire, ou Contr'un*, ed. Simone Goyard-Fabre (Paris: GF Flammarion, 1983).

An etching of the house in Sarlat-la-Canéda where La Boétie was born. From the frontispiece to Paul Bonnefon's, *Oeuvres complètes* of La Boétie, 1892.

ÉTIENNE DE LA BOÉTIE

Discourse on Voluntary Servitude (or Against One)[1]

> *I see no good in having several masters:*
> *Let one, not more, be master, and one alone be king.*[2]

Homer's Ulysses said this, speaking in public. Had he said nothing else than

> *I see no good in having several masters,*

it would have been just as well said, with nothing else. But instead of saying, to speak sensibly, that domination by several masters could not be good, since the power of a single man once he takes on this title of "master" is harsh and unreasonable, he went and added, on the contrary,

> *Let one, not more, be master, and one alone be king.*

No doubt Ulysses should be excused, since possibly it was necessary for him to use this language to calm the army's revolt, suiting his words more to the time than to the truth, I think. But speaking with all consideration, it is a profound misfortune to be subject to one master, who you can never be sure will be good, since it is always in his power to be bad when he wishes to; and to have several masters means that the more one has, the more chances

---

1. The phrase is reminiscent of one in Seneca, "On the Shortness of Life" (*De brevitate vitae*), 2.1, where he writes of those "who are worn out by voluntary servitude (*voluntaria servitute*) in a thankless attendance upon the great." The end of Pausanias' speech in Plato, *Symposium*, 184c–184d may also be relevant; there the phrase is "willing bondage" (Loeb), "voluntary service" (Jowett), and "willing subjugation" (Nehamas and Woodruff; see Introduction, n. 34).

2. The quotation is from a French translation of Homer, *Iliad*, 2.204–5. Critics convinced that the *Discourse* is a rhetorical exercise reinforce their argument by highlighting all its classical sources and allusions.

one has for profound misfortune. So I do not wish at the present time to open the much-debated question as to whether other kinds of republics are better than a monarchy.[3] Moreover, before questioning what rank the monarchy should have among republics, I should like to know whether it should have any, since it is hard to believe that there is anything "public" in this government, where everything belongs to one man. But that question is reserved for another time and would indeed require a separate treatise, or rather would open up all kinds of political discussion.[4]

At this time I would only wish to understand how it happens that so many men, so many towns, so many cities, so many nations at times tolerate a single tyrant who has no other power than what they grant him, who has no other ability to harm them than inasmuch as they are willing to tolerate it, who could do ill to them only insofar as they would rather suffer it than oppose him.[5] It is certainly quite something,[6] and yet so common that one must

---

3. Among many other classical sources, see Aristotle, *Politics*, 3.7–8, 1279a22–1280a6; Plato, *Politics*, 291c–292d; *Laws*, 712c; 714b; Plutarch, *Moralia* 10 ("On Monarchy, Democracy, and Oligarchy"), 826a–827c; and Xenophon, *Cyropaedia*, I, 1. For a French Renaissance connection, see Joachim du Bellay's poem *Ample discours au Roy sur le faict des quatre Estats du royaume de France* by Joachim Du Bellay; for more on him and the Pléiade, see n. 76. Generally speaking, the operative distinction for this question granted that one person ruled in both a monarchy and a tyranny but termed the former legitimate and the latter not.

4. We have no way of knowing whether any of La B's lost works might have dealt with this "much-debated question."

5. Lucan, *De bello civili (Pharsalia)*, 4.185 is a possible source for La B's concern: *Usque adeone times, quem tu facis ipse timendum?* ("Do you fear so greatly the leader whom you alone make fear-inspiring?") Lucan has Caesar pose this question to his troops in Spain during the summer of 49 BCE when fighting the Pompeian army led by Afranius and Petreius. Caesar is trying to prevent their escape; this question is supposed to fire up his troops. The force of the question rests on the ax Lucan has to grind: he dislikes Caesar's passion for sole power and contrasts it with the willingness of Afranius and Petreius to share command jointly.

6. A section several pages long, resembling a version (it is often verbatim) of *Voluntary Servitude* printed in the *Réville-matin des François* published in Paris in 1574, begins here.

feel more sorrow than amazement, to see a million men serving miserably, with their necks under the yoke, not compelled by *force majeure* but seemingly rather charmed and enchanted by the mere name of one whose power they should not fear since he is alone, nor should they love his qualities since he acts cruelly and inhumanely toward them. The weakness among men like us is such that we must often obey force: we need to play for time, we cannot always get the upper hand. So if a nation is obliged by war to serve one man, like the city of Athens with the Thirty Tyrants, we should not be surprised that it does serve but be sorry for the incident, or rather be neither surprised nor sorry, but bear the evil patiently and wait for better fortune in the future.[7]

Such is our nature that the ordinary duties of friendship take up a good part of the course of our lives.[8] It is reasonable to love virtue, to admire fine deeds, to recognize those by whom we have been given benefits and often to lessen our own pleasure, so as to increase the honor and advantage of someone we love and who deserves it. And so if the inhabitants of a country have found some great figure who has offered them proof of great foresight for their protection, great boldness in their defense, great concern to govern them, if from then on they consent to obey and put their trust in him to the extent of granting him some advantages, I do not know whether it would be a wise thing, given that they take him away from a place where he did good to put him where he may do ill; but certainly it could not fail to be a good thing not to fear ill from someone from whom one has received nothing but good.

---

7. The reign of the Thirty Tyrants lasted a year after Athens' defeat in the Peloponnesian War, until democracy was restored in 403 BCE. See Xenophon, *The Hellenica*, 2.3–4; and Seneca the Younger, "On Tranquility of Mind" (*De tranquillitate animi*), 5.1–3, with its question: "Could the city in which there were as many tyrants as there might be satellites ever find peace?" which suggests the main thrust of La B's argument here.

8. See Aristotle, *Nicomachean Ethics*, 8.1.3; and Cicero, *On Friendship (De amicitia)*, 5.19–20, 8.27. The question of friendship will come up again when he discusses the incompatibility of tyrants and friendship. See Floyd Gray, "Montaigne's Friends" for a discussion of the similarity of both men's position on friendship, based on their reading of chapters 8 and 9 in the *Nicomachean Ethics*.

But good Lord! . . . what can that be? How will we say what that is called? What kind of misfortune is that? What vice, or rather what unfortunate vice, to see a countless number of people not obeying but serving; not being governed but tyrannized; with neither property, nor relations, wives, nor children, nor even their lives belonging to them; enduring pillage, lechery, cruelty, not from an army, not from a barbarian camp against which they ought to shed their blood and their lives in the struggle, but from just one man, not from a Hercules or a Samson, but from a single puny man, and generally the most cowardly, effeminate one in the nation, accustomed not to the dust of battle but at the very most to the sand of the jousting field; one not capable of commanding men by force, but hardly capable of basely serving the least little woman.[9] Shall we call this cowardice? Shall we say that those who serve are cowards and toadies? If two, three, or four do not defend themselves against one, that is strange, but still possible—indeed, one can then say that it is for lack of courage. But if a hundred or a thousand tolerate one single man, can we not say that they do not want, not that they do not dare, to deal with him, and that this is not cowardice but disdain or scorn? If we see not a hundred, not a thousand men, but a hundred towns, a thousand cities, a million men not assail a single man, when the best treated one of them all has had the evil of being a serf and a slave, what shall we call that? Is it cowardice? Now there is naturally a limit to any vice beyond which they cannot go: two, possibly ten, can fear one—but if a thousand, a million, a thousand cities, do not defend themselves against one, that is not cowardice, it cannot go that far, any more than bravery extends to a single man scaling a fortress, attacking an army, conquering a kingdom. So what bizarre kind of vice is this, which does not yet deserve the title of cowardice, which does not find any name base enough, which nature disavows making and language refuses to name?

Put fifty thousand armed men on one side, as many on the other, arrange them in battle formation, let them meet in combat, one side free men fighting for their freedom, the others to take it away.

---

9. Some critics, who would see allusions to contemporary France, and thus a later date for the *Discourse* than 1548–1549, see this as an allusion to King François I (reigned 1559–1560).

Which ones will we predict victory for, which ones do we think will go to battle more bravely: those who hope to keep their liberty as a reward for their efforts, or those who can expect no other pay for the blows they give or receive than servitude to another? The former always have before their eyes the joy of past life, the expectation of such happiness in the future. They do not remember the small hardship they experience for the time of a battle so much as what they—and their children and all posterity—will be able to experience. The others have nothing to embolden them but a little tingle of greed that stops up suddenly in the face of danger, and cannot be so burning, it seems, as not to be extinguished by the slightest drop of blood from their wounds. In the well-known battles of Miltiades, Leonidas, and Themistocles, which were fought two thousand years ago and are still as fresh in the memory of books and men today as if it been only yesterday, which were fought in Greece for the benefit of the Greeks and as an example to all, what do you think gave as few men as the Greeks were not the ability, but the courage to withstand the force of so many ships that the sea was filled with them, to defeat so many nations that, if they had needed to, the army of the Greeks would not have provided enough captains for their enemies' armies?—nothing, it would seem, except that in those glorious days it was not so much the battle of Greeks against Persians as the victory of liberty over domination, of freedom over greed.[10]

It is strange to hear people speak of the courage liberty instills in the hearts of those defending it. But something done in every country, by all men, every day—for one man to abuse a hundred thousand and deprive them of their liberty: who would believe it if he only heard about it and did not see it? And if it were done only in strange countries and distant lands, and someone told of it, who would not think that was fictitious and invented rather than true? Yet this lone tyrant does not have to be fought, there is no need to defeat him: he is defeated by himself if the country does not accept its

---

10. Miltiades conquered the Persians, ruled by Darius, at the battle of Marathon in 490 BCE; in 480 BCE the Persians, led by Xerxes, were defeated at the battle of the pass of Thermopylae when Leonidas and three hundred Spartans refused to retreat and were annihilated; later that year Themistocles defeated Xerxes' fleet at the battle of Salamis.

servitude.[11] Nothing must be taken from him; but he must be given nothing. The country does not need to go to the trouble of doing anything for itself, as long as it does nothing against itself. Thus it is the people themselves who let themselves be—or rather get themselves—abused, since if they ceased being slaves they would be rid of it. It is the people who enslave themselves, who cut their own throats, who, when they have the choice of being either free men or slaves, give up their freedom and take up the yoke if they accept their ill, or rather pursue it.[12] If it cost them anything to recover their liberty, I would not urge them to do so—though what ought a man to hold dearer than regaining his natural right and, as it were, becoming a man, not a beast, once again? But yet I do not desire such great boldness in him, I allow him to prefer some certainty of living miserably to a dubious hope of living happily. Why, if all it takes to have liberty is to desire it, if nothing is needed but the simple will, is there any nation on earth that deems it still too costly when it can be won by a mere wish, and scants its will to recover a boon that it ought to redeem with its blood, when all honorable men, if they have lost it, must deem life objectionable and death beneficial? Certainly, as the flame of a small spark grows and keeps getting stronger, and the more wood it finds the more it is ready to burn unless water is poured on it to put it out, and only if no more wood is put on it, so that having no more to consume it consumes itself and becomes weak and no longer fire—so with tyrants, the more they pillage, the more they demand, the more they ruin and destroy, the more they are granted, the more they are served, the stronger they grow and they keep on getting stronger and more able to demolish and destroy everything. And if they are not granted anything, if they are not obeyed, without fighting, without a blow being struck, they are left naked and defeated, and are no longer anything—but like the root when it has no more liquid or food, the branch dries up and dies.

---

11. M echoes this idea when he discussed the need to say no. See "The Education of Children," I, 26 [25], with its connection to Plutarch, *Moralia* 7 ("On Compliancy"), 532e–f; and *Selected Essays*, ed. Atkinson and Sices, pp. lvi–lvii, 51. La B returns to this point in the discussion starting on p. 30: "But now I come to a point that, to my mind, is the source and secret of domination, the basis and foundation of tyranny."

12. Many of these images can be found in Dio Chrysostom, *Discourses* 80, ("On Freedom").

Nothing more important
to preserve than liberty

Bold men do not fear danger to get what they demand, sensible men do not avoid effort; cowards and dullards do not know either how to withstand ill or how to recover what is theirs: they get no farther than wishing for it, and because of their cowardice they lose the power to recover it. The desire to have it remains in them by nature: this desire, this will is common to wise men and fools, to brave men and cowards, to wish for everything that, once acquired, would make them happy and content. There is one thing about which it has to be said, for some reason, nature does not make men yearn for it: once liberty, which is nonetheless so great and pleasing a boon, is lost, all ills follow one upon the other, and even the good things remaining completely lose their taste and savor, ruined by servitude. Liberty alone apparently is not yearned for by men, not for any other reason than that if they yearned for it they would have it—as if they refused to make this fine acquisition because it is too easy.

Poor, miserable, foolish peoples, nations stubborn in your ill and blind to your good! You let the finest and greatest part of your wealth be carried off under your noses, your fields be plundered, your houses be robbed and stripped of heirlooms and furniture, you live in such a fashion that you cannot boast anything belongs to you, and it would seem you would be happy today to have just a share in your property, your families, and your lives. And all this waste, this misfortune, this ruin comes to you not from your enemies, but indeed from the enemy, the one you make as great as he is, for whom you go to war so bravely, for whose grandeur you do not refuse to offer yourselves up to die. The man who has such mastery over you has but two eyes, has but two hands, has but one body, and has nothing more than what the least man in the great, infinite number of our cities has, except the advantage you give him to destroy you. Where did he get so many eyes to spy on you, if you are not granting them to him?[13] How does he have so many hands to strike you, if he does not get them from you? Where does he get the feet that he tramples your cities with, if they are not yours? How does he have any power over you, if not from you? How would he dare to attack you, if he did not have your agreement? What could he do to you, if you were not fences for the thief who robs you, accomplices of the murderer who kills you, and traitors to yourselves? You sow your crops so he may lay waste

---

13. See Erasmus, *Adagia* LB II 69 D.

to them. You furnish and fill your houses to provide for his plunders. You raise your daughters so he can satisfy his lust. You raise your children so that the best he can do with them is to take them off to his wars, to lead them to slaughter, to have them minister to his lusts and carry out his vendettas. You work yourselves to the bone so that he can indulge in his delights and wallow in his filthy, nasty pleasures. You weaken yourselves in order to make him stronger and stricter in keeping you on a shorter rein. And you can deliver yourselves from so many indignities that the very beasts would either not feel or not endure, if you try, not to deliver yourselves from them but merely to wish to do so. Resolve no longer to be slaves and you are free! I do not want you to push him or overthrow him, but merely no longer to sustain him and, like a great colossus whose base has been pulled away, you will see him collapse of his own weight and break up.[14]

But physicians certainly do advise not trying to deal with incurable wounds, and it is not wise for me to try to preach about this to people who lost consciousness of it long ago.[15] As they no longer feel their ill, it is obvious that their disease is terminal. Let us therefore seek to guess if we can how this stubborn willingness to serve has become so deeply rooted thus, that it now seems the very love of liberty is not so natural.

First of all, I believe it is beyond doubt that if we lived with the rights that Nature has granted us and teachings she imparts, we would be naturally obedient to our parents, subject to reason, and slaves to no one. Of the obedience that everyone has to his father and mother, with no other prompting than from his nature, all men bear witness, each for himself. As to whether reason is innate or not (a question thoroughly debated by academics, and touched on by every school of philosophers), as of this time I do not think I would be wrong to say that there is in our soul some natural seed of reason that, if fostered by good counsel and custom, flowers into virtue[16] and

---

14. The image occurs in Plutarch, *Moralia* 10 ("Precepts of Statecraft"), 779f–780c. The passage from the 1574 publication of the *Réveille-matin des François* ends here.

15. Based on Hippocrates quoted by Cicero, *Letters to Atticus*, 426 (16.15.) 5.

16. See Cicero, *On Ends (De finibus bonorum et malorum)*, 2.14.45 for this standard Stoic image and doctrine. La B returns to this image; see n. 31. The word *academics* might also refer to the Platonic doctrines of Plato's Academy.

on the other hand often is stifled and dies out because it cannot endure against vices that arise.[17] But certainly, if there is anything clear and evident in Nature and that we must not be blind to, it is that Nature, God's minister and man's tutor, has made us all in the same form and, it would seem, the same mold so we might look upon one another as comrades or rather as brothers. And if in apportioning the gifts she gave us Nature gave more benefits of either body or mind to some men and less to others, still she did not intend to put us in this world as in an enclosed field, and did not send the stronger or cleverer ones down like armed brigands in the forest to bully the weaker ones there. But it is rather to be thought that in giving a greater share to some and a lesser one to others, she wanted to make room for brotherly love so it would be of use, with some having the power to give aid, the others the need to receive it. Therefore, since this good mother[18] has given to us all the whole world as our home, lodged us all more or less in the same house, designed us all on the same pattern so that each one may see and pretty much recognize himself in the other, if she has given us all the great gift of speech and words for us to get to know each other better and be better friends,[19] and by the common, mutual declaration of our thoughts to bring about a communion of our wills, and if she has striven by every means so to tighten and strengthen the bonds of our union and society, if she has shown in all things that she wanted to make us not so much united as all one, there cannot be any doubt that we are all naturally free, since we are all comrades. And it cannot be understood by anyone that Nature put any in servitude since she put us all into one company.

But the truth is that it is fruitless to debate whether liberty is natural, since no one can be kept in servitude without wronging him, and there is nothing in the world as contrary to Nature, which is entirely reasonable, as injustice. It therefore remains that liberty is natural, and by the same token, in my opinion, that we are born not only in possession of our freedom but with the desire to defend it.[20] Now if by chance we should have any doubt of that and are

---

17. See Cicero, *Tusculan Disputations*, 2.5.13.

18. I.e., Nature.

19. Cf. Cicero, *On the Nature of the Gods*, 2.59.148.

20. A succinct statement of the essay's starting point, La B's basic assumption

so degenerate that we cannot recognize our possessions or, apparently, our natural desires, I shall have to give you the honor you possess, and so to speak put the beasts up in the pulpit to teach you your nature and condition. The beasts, God help me, cry out to men, if they do not close their ears, "Long live liberty!" A number of them die as soon as they are captured. Just as a fish leaves life as soon as it leaves the water, so they leave the light and will not outlive their natural freedom. If some among the animals had preeminence, these would become their nobility. When the others, from the greatest to the smallest, are captured, they put up so great a resistance with claws, horns, beaks, and feet that they show quite well how dear they hold what they are losing; then when they are captured, they show us so many clear signs that they realize their misfortune, it is easy to see that thenceforth they are languishing more than they are living, and that they go on living more to lament their lost happiness than to take pleasure in servitude. What does the elephant mean, when after defending itself to the point of exhaustion, seeing there is nothing left to do and it is about to be taken, it sinks its jaws and breaks its teeth against the trees,[21] other than that its great desire to remain free gives it wit and counsels it to bargain with the hunters whether it will be let off for the price of its teeth and be allowed to offer up its ivory to pay a ransom for its liberty? We cajole a horse from the time of its birth to accustom it to service, and yet we can never flatter it so well that it does not champ at the bit and rear up against the spur when the time comes to break it, as if to show Nature, it seems, and at least testify thus that, if it serves, it is not willingly but rather under constraint from us.[22] What shall we say, then?

> Even oxen groan under the weight of the yoke,
> And birds in their cages complain,

and the source of wonder and despair that people so willingly sign over this freedom to others, especially a tyrant.

21. See Pliny, *Natural History (Naturalis historia)*, 8.4.8.

22. See M, "Physiognomy," III, 12, *Selected Essays*, ed. Atkinson and Sices, p. 212: "How fine it is to see that . . . our wisdom draws from the very beasts the most useful teachings for the greatest and most essential aspects of our lives." This point is made often in Xenophon, *Cyropaedia*. See also Plutarch, *Moralia* 12 ("Beasts Are Rational"), 985d–992e.

other animals die when see their liberty is going to be taken away

as I once said, passing the time with our French poetry—for in writing to you, Longa,[23] I shall not be afraid to mingle some of my verse, since I never read it to you but you make me quite proud by the appearance you give of enjoying it. And so—since all things that have feeling, by that very fact feel the pain of subjection and pursue liberty; since even the animals that are made to serve man can be accustomed to serving only under protest of a contrary desire—what misfortune can have so denatured man, the only one truly born to live in freedom, and make him lose the memory of his original being, and the desire to regain it?

There are three kinds of tyrants:[24] the first hold royal power through election by the people, the next by force of arms, and the last by family succession. Those who have acquired it as a spoil of war behave in such a way that they are indeed known to be (as they say) in conquered territory. The ones who are born kings are usually no better; rather, since they were born and raised in the bosom of tyranny, they suck the tyrant's nature with their milk, and regard the people who are under them as their hereditary slaves.[25] And depending on the nature they are most inclined to—miserly or wasteful—however they are, they treat the kingdom like their inheritance. The one to whom the people have given the state ought to be more tolerable, I think; and I believe he would be, except that upon seeing himself raised above the rest, flattered by something or other called "grandeur," he decides never to give it up: usually that man declares he will hand over to his children the power the people granted him. And once these men have gotten that idea, it is amazing how much they surpass the other tyrants in all sorts of vice and even in cruelty, since they see no other means to strengthen the new tyranny than to extend servitude so far, and so alienate their subjects from liberty that, although the

---

23. Guillaume de Lur-Longa was La B's predecessor in the Bordeaux *Parlement*, a trusted older friend, and, from these words, would appear to be the dedicatee of this treatise. These lines have not been found in the poems of La B that M later published.

24. Whoever copied de Mesmes' manuscript omitted several important words: "I am talking about bad princes" (*je parle des meschans princes*); Gontarbert edition, p. 93. Consequently, not all monarchs are ipso facto bad.

25. La B rejects a distinction, based on Aristotle, *Politics*, 3.7.5, between king and tyrant that most of his contemporaries accepted.

memory of it is fresh, they can make them forget it. So to tell the truth I do see some difference, but I do not see there is any choice between them. And although the means of coming to power may differ, still the way they exercise it is just about the same. Those elected treat them as if they had taken on bulls to tame; the conquerors treat them as their prey; the successors think to treat them as their natural slaves.

(In this connection, however, if by chance some entirely new people—neither accustomed to subjection nor enticed by liberty—were to be born today and they did not know what either one or the other was, or scarcely even the words; if they were offered the choice of living as serfs or as free men according to laws they would agree on, there can be no doubt that they would much prefer obeying reason alone rather than serving some man.)Except possibly if they were those of Israel who took a tyrant upon themselves without compulsion or necessity;[26] I have never read the story of those people without feeling great annoyance, almost to the point of becoming inhumane and rejoicing in the many ills that came to them from that. But certainly all men, as long as they have anything human in them, before they let themselves be subjected, would have to be either compelled or deceived: compelled by a foreign army, like Sparta or Athens by Alexander's forces,[27] or by factions, such as the Athenian oligarchy had become earlier in the hands of Pisistratus.[28] They often lose their liberty through deception, and they are not enticed into this by someone else so often as they are deceived by themselves. In this way the people of Syracuse, the leading city in Sicily (I am told in our day it is called Saragossa[29]), when pressed by wars, rashly looking only to the present danger, named Dionysius as first tyrant and put

---

26. See 1 Samuel 9–10; Douay, Kings I (Samuel's anointment of Saul as king of Israel).

27. Alexander the Great became ruler of all Greece in 335 BCE: see Plutarch, *Life of Alexander*, 11–14.

28. Pisistratus, the chief of the democratic faction in Athens, became tyrant of the city in 546 BCE and remained in power until 527 BCE. See Plutarch, *Life of Solon*, 29–31.

29. In fact, in Sicilian dialect Syracuse is called *Sarausa*, not Saragossa. It is named for a large marsh, formerly known as the Syraca, now Il Pantano, one of the city's best defenses against attack. Dionysius the Elder became tyrant, and led the war against Carthage, in the early fourth century BCE; see Diodorus Siculus, *Library of History*, 12–13.

him in charge of the army; they did not watch out, once they had made him so important, and so this fine fellow returned victorious—as if he had defeated not his enemies but his fellow citizens—and from commander he made himself king, and from king tyrant.

It is unbelievable how people, once they are subjected, fall so quickly into such a deep forgetfulness of freedom that it is impossible for them to reawaken and regain it; they serve so freely and so willingly that you would say to see them that they had not lost their liberty but won their servitude. It is true that in the beginning one serves, constrained and defeated by force; but those that come after serve without regret, and do willingly what those who came before did under constraint. That is because men born under the yoke, and then raised and nurtured in serfdom, are content to live as they were born, without looking any farther; not thinking they have any other possessions or rights than what they have found, they take the state of their birth for their nature. And yet no heir is so prodigal and nonchalant that he does not take a look at his father's account-books, sometimes, to see whether he is enjoying all the rights of his inheritance and if anything has been taken from him or his predecessor. But certainly custom, which has great power over us in all things, exerts in no other area so great a force as this: teaching us to serve and, as Mithridates was said to have grown used to drinking poison,[30] teaching us to swallow the toxin of servitude and not find it at all bitter. We cannot deny that Nature has a great role in pulling us where it wishes and getting us called well- or ill-bred. But it must still be confessed that it has less power over us than does custom; for nature, no matter how good, is lost if it is not sustained, and nurture always fashions us after itself, even though it may be despite Nature. The seeds of good that Nature sows in us are so tiny and slippery that they cannot withstand the slightest clash with opposing nurture.[31] They are not maintained as easily as they are corrupted, dissolved, and reduced to naught, any more or less than fruit trees, all of which have some other nature that they hold on to if they are left alone, but that they abandon right away to bear other, alien fruit, not their own, as they are grafted.

---

30. See Aulus Gellius, *Attic Nights* (*Noctes Atticae*), 17.16.2.

31. For the source of this image, see n. 16.

Each herb has its properties, its nature and individuality, and yet frost, weather, soil, or the gardener's hand add or take away much of their quality from them: it is hard to recognize a plant one has seen in one place somewhere else.

Anyone seeing the Venetians—a handful of people living so freely that the meanest among them would not want to be king of them all, born and nurtured so, that they recognize no ambition but to see who will best counsel and take care to preserve liberty, taught and formed so, from infancy on, that they would not take the rest of earthly felicities if they lost the least bit of their freedom[32]—as I say, would anyone who saw those people and then went off from there to the lands of the one we call the "Great Lord,"[33] and saw the people there who wish to be born only to serve him, and who give up their lives to maintain his power, think that these and the others had the same nature? Would he not rather judge that, leaving a city of men, he had entered a zoological garden? Lycurgus,[34] the lawgiver of Sparta, had raised two dogs they say, both of the same litter, both suckled on the same milk, one fattened in the kitchen, the other one accustomed to the sound of the horn and the cornet in the field. Wishing to show the Spartans that men are what their nurture makes them, he put the two dogs in the middle of the marketplace and between them a soup and a hare; one ran to the dish and the other to the hare. "And yet the two are indeed brothers," he said. So that man nurtured and formed the Spartans so well with his laws and his government that

---

32. M noted that La B "would rather have been born in Venice than in Sarlat—and rightly so," "Friendship," I, 28 [27], *Selected Essays*, ed. Atkinson and Sices, p. 86. It has been suggested that Machiavelli's positive thoughts about the Venetian republic in his *Florentine Histories* could have contributed to this passage, though Venetian doges were not known for letting people live "so freely."

33. I.e., the sultan of the Ottoman Empire, who was also known as the "Grand Turk," whom contemporaries generally considered the epitome of a tyrant.

34. Lycurgus (800?–730? BCE), the legendary lawgiver of Sparta, established the military-oriented reformation of Spartan society in accordance with the Oracle of Apollo at Delphi. For the following anecdote, see Plutarch, *Moralia* 3 ("Sayings of Spartans"), 225f–226a. Du Bellay's poem *Ample discours au Roy*, referred to in n. 3, also uses this anecdote.

each of them would rather have died a thousand deaths than recognize any other ruler than law and reason.[35]

I take pleasure in recalling an exchange long ago between one of the favorites of Xerxes, the great king of Persia, and Spartans. When Xerxes was preparing his great army to conquer Greece, he sent his ambassadors around the Grecian cities to demand water and earth: that was how the Persians summoned cities to surrender to them. He did not send to Athens or to Sparta because, of those that his father, Darius, had sent there, some had been thrown into ditches by the Athenians and Spartans, others into wells, and they been told to go boldly and get water and earth from there to bring to their prince. Those people could not tolerate their liberty being affected by even the slightest word. Because they had acted that way, the Spartans learned they had incurred the hatred of the gods, in particular of Talthybius, the god of heralds. To pacify them, they decided to send two of their citizens to appear before Xerxes, for him to do as he saw fit with them and thus be compensated for his father's ambassadors whom they had killed. Two Spartans, one named Sperthias and the other Bulis, volunteered to go and make this payment. They did indeed go and along the way arrived at the palace of a Persian named Hydarnes, who was the king's deputy in all the cities of Asia on the seacoast. He received them with great favor and gave a banquet for them; after each one let fall several remarks, he asked them why they so refused the king's friendship. He said, "Spartans, you may see and know by me how capable the king is of honoring those who deserve it; if you were his, you may think that he would do the same for you. If you were his and he met you, neither one of you would fail to be lord of a Greek city." "Hydarnes, in this you cannot give us good advice," said the Spartans, "because you have experienced the boon you promise us, but you do not know the one that we enjoy. You have enjoyed the king's favor, but you know nothing of liberty: what it tastes like, how sweet it is. For had you tasted of it, you yourself would counsel us to defend it—not with lance and shield but with tooth and nail."[36] That

---

35. Some manuscripts read "law and the king" (*la loi et le Roy*); Gontarbert edition, p. 98.

36. See Herodotus, *The Persian Wars*, 7.133–37; see also Erasmus, *Adagia*, LB II 655 C–D and 160 B–C.

Spartan said what needed to be said, but certainly both of them spoke as they had been nurtured. For it was not possible for the Persian, never having had it, to miss liberty, or for the Spartans to endure subjection once they had tasted freedom.

When Cato of Utica was still a child and under the rod, he often came and went at Sulla the dictator's house—both because the door was never barred to him, thanks to the place and family he was from, and also because they were close relations. He always had his tutor when he went there, as was usual with children of good family. He noted that at Sulla's lodging, in his presence or under his orders, some were imprisoned, others were condemned, one was banished, another strangled, one demanded a citizen's sequestration, another his head: in sum, everything there was done, not as in a city official's home but as in a tyrant of the people's, and it was not a court of justice but a workshop of tyranny. So this young lad said to his tutor: "Why not give me a dagger? I shall hide it under my toga. I often go into Sulla's bedroom before he is up; my arm is strong enough to rid the city of him." These words certainly befitted Cato. It was a beginning for that figure worthy of his death. And nonetheless if one mentions neither his name nor his country and relates just the deed, the thing will speak for itself, and chances are that people will judge it was a Roman, born in Rome[37] and while it was free.[38] Why do I mention all this? Certainly not because I deem that the land or the soil have anything to do with it—for in every country, in every clime, subjection is bitter and being free is agreeable—but because I deem that those who have found a yoke on their necks at birth are to be pitied. They should be either excused or pardoned if, not having seen even the shadow of liberty and not being at all aware of it, they cannot perceive how bad it is for them to be slaves. If there were some

---

37. At this point some manuscripts indicate the addition of "but in the true Rome" (dedans Rome, mais dedans *la vraye Rome*); Gontarbert edition, p. 101. Goyard-Fabre interprets this change to mean Rome before Sulla's dictatorship.

38. See Plutarch, *Life of Cato the Younger*, 3; Plutarch notes that Cato, 95–46 BCE, was fourteen years old when this incident occurred. M uses Cato's example in a similar context, see "Cruelty," II, 11, and "Physiognomy," III, 12, *Selected Essays*, ed. Atkinson and Sices, pp. 129, 199–200.

country where, as Homer says of the Cimmerians,[39] the sun appears different than it does to us and, after shining on them continuously for six months, leaves them to sleep in darkness without coming back to see them for the other half-year, should we be surprised if those who were born during that long night, not having heard about daylight and never having seen the sun shine, grew used to the darkness in which they were born and did not desire the light?[40] We do not complain about what we have never had, and we only miss what has given us pleasure; and the remembrance of past joy always accompanies the realization of ill. The nature of man is to be free and to wish to be so; but his nature also is such that he follows naturally the bent given him by his nurture.

So let us say, therefore, that everything that man is nurtured by and accustomed to is more or less natural to him, but only what his simple, unaltered nature calls him to is really innate in him. Thus the first reason for voluntary servitude is custom: just as with the stoutest short-tailed steeds, which in the beginning champ at the bit, and then make light of it, and though until recently they reared up against the saddle, now they show off in harness and take pride in their armor. People say they have always been subjected, that is how their forefathers lived. They think they are required to endure the ill, and convince themselves by examples, and they themselves base possession by those who tyrannize them on the length of time. But in truth, years never give a right to do ill: rather, they increase the injustice.[41] Yet there are always some, better born than the others, who feel the weight of the yoke and cannot help shaking it, who never grow used to subjection, and who always— like Ulysses, who on land and on sea always sought the smoke of his

---

39. The Cimmerians were ancient equestrian nomads of Indo-European origin. According to Herodotus, they inhabited the region north of the Caucasus and the Black Sea, in what is now the Ukraine and Russia, in the eighth and seventh centuries BCE.

40. See Homer, *Odyssey*, 11.11–19.

41. Goyard-Fabre, in her edition of *Discours de la servitude volontaire*, p. 151, n. 56, points out that, to challenge those who would base law solely on custom or tradition, La B uses the word *injustice* in the etymological sense of *in-juria*, "the absence of law."

home[42]—cannot help looking to their natural privileges and recalling their predecessors and their original state. It is often they who, having clear understanding and a perceptive mind, are not content like the ordinary people just to look immediately before their feet[43] if they do not see what is ahead and behind, and also not to recall past things to judge those of the future and to measure present ones. They are men whose heads are well-made to start with, who have refined them by study and learning. These men, even if liberty were completely lost and absent from the world, would imagine it and feel it in their minds and still savor it; servitude is not to their taste, no matter how it is dressed up.

The Grand Turk[44] indeed took note of the fact that books and doctrine, more than anything else, give men sense and understanding to know themselves and hate tyranny.[45] I understand that he has scarcely any learned people in his lands, nor does he ask for any. In general, now, the good zeal and emotion of those who have retained their devotion to freedom in spite of time—though they may be numerous—has no effect, because they do not know each other. Under a tyrant they are deprived of their liberty to act, to speak, and almost to think: in their imagination they all become individuals.[46] So Momus, the god of mockery, was not mocking when he found

---

42. See Homer, *Odyssey*, 1.57–59; see also Erasmus, *Adagia*, LB II 76 C–D. Du Bellay uses this famous passage in the second stanza of his frequently anthologized poem, "Heureux qui, comme Ulysse, a fait un beau voyage" (*Regrets*, 31). For more on Du Bellay and the Pléiade, see n. 76.

43. See Terence, *Adelphoe*, 385–87, and Erasmus, *Adagia*, LB II 888 A–C.

44. See n. 33.

45. It is ironic that praise for "books" that "more than anything else, give men sense and understanding to know themselves and hate tyranny" should come from someone who published nothing, no book, during his lifetime. And those of his "relics" that M published in 1571 were not necessarily his most important ones.

46. Aristotle, *Politics*, 5.9.2, points out that a tactic of tyrants is to isolate their people, whereas both La B and M believe, in M's words in "The Education of Children," I, 26 [25], that "Good governments make sure they assemble the citizens and bring them together for sports and games, as they do for serious religious ceremonies: they enhance civic spirit and friendship"; *Selected Essays*, ed. Atkinson and Sices, p. 72.

grounds to criticize the man made by Vulcan because he had not put a little window into his heart whereby his thoughts can be seen.[47] It has indeed been said that Brutus, Cassius, and Casca, when they undertook the deliverance of Rome—or rather of the entire world—did not want Cicero, a great zealot of public welfare if there ever was one, to be in on it. They deemed his heart too weak for such a great deed: they did trust his will, but they were not at all certain of his courage.[48] And yet if anyone looks into the actions of past times and the ancient annals, he will find few or none who, seeing their country ill led and in the wrong hands, undertook with good, whole, and unfeigned intent to deliver it and did not succeed, and that liberty, to shine forth, did not itself lend a hand. Harmodius, Aristogeiton, Thrasybulus, Brutus the Elder, Valerius, and Dion,[49] as they thought virtuously of it, carried it out successfully: in

---

47. See the dialogue by Lucian, "The Rival Philosophies" (*Hermotimus*), 20; see also Erasmus, *Adagia*, LB II 210 D–E.

48. See Plutarch, *Life of Cicero*, 42, but the lack of "courage" is also apparent in his *Life of Brutus*. In *Julius Caesar*, act I, scene 3, Shakespeare has Cicero appear briefly with no comment on the current political scene. In contrast to Casca's dire explanation of the "portentous" natural phenomena, Cicero points out with cool rationality, if not skepticism, that "Indeed, it is a strange-disposed time: / But men may construe things, after their fashion, / Clean from the purpose of the things themselves." In act I, scene 2, Brutus thinks he is disturbed by Caesar's actions but in act II, scene 1, either because he doubts his courage or dislikes his vanity, he opts for excluding Cicero "For he will never follow any thing / That other men begin (151–52).

49. M also alludes to Harmodius and Aristogeiton in "Friendship," I, 28 [27]. Based on Pausanias' long speech in Plato, *Symposium*, 180d–185c, they were Athenian male lovers who, out of hatred of tyranny, sought to end the dictatorship of Hippias, Hipparchus' brother, by assassinating Hipparchus in 514 BCE. They were betrayed and tortured to death, but many Athenians, though not Herodotus, believed they paved the way for the tyrant's downfall in 511; Herodotus, *Persian Wars*, 5.55, 6.109, 6.123. Thucydides, *Peloponnesian War*, 6.53–59, notes that Aristogeiton's motive really was fear that Hipparchus would steal Harmodius' affections. Thrasybulus (d. 388 BCE) was an Athenian general and democratic leader; he led a group of exiles to oust the Thirty Tyrants (n. 7) from power. In 411 BCE, in the wake of an oligarchic coup in Athens, the pro-democracy sailors at Samos elected him as a general, making him a primary leader of the successful democratic resistance to that coup; Xenophon, *The Hellenica*, 2.4. Lucius Junius Brutus was the

such cases fortune almost never fails good will. Brutus the Younger
and Cassius were quite successful in doing away with servitude, but in
restoring liberty they died, not miserably (for what blasphemy it would
be to say there was anything miserable in either the life or the death
of those men!), but to the great detriment, the enduring misfortune,
and the total ruin of the republic, which appears to have been bur-
ied along with them.[50] The other attempts made later against Roman
emperors were just conspiracies of ambitious people who are not to
be pitied for the problems that befell them, since it is easy to see that
they desired not to take away, but to move the crown while claiming
to overthrow the tyrant, and to retain the tyranny. I should not myself
have wished better success for them, and am happy that they showed
by their example that the holy name of liberty must not be misused for
a bad undertaking.

But to return to our subject, which I had almost lost sight of, the
primary reason why men serve willingly is because they are born serfs
and are raised as such. From this there arises another one: under tyrants
people easily grow weak and unmanly. For this I am deeply indebted
to Hippocrates, who took note of it and said so in one of his books
that he wrote on diseases.[51] That figure definitely had his heart always
in the right place, and he indeed showed it when the great king[52] tried
to attract him with offers and great presents: he answered frankly

---

founder of the Roman Republic, and traditionally one of the first consuls, in
509 BCE. He overthrew the tyrannical rule of Tarquinius Superbus in 510.
He was the ancestor of the Junius family in ancient Rome, including Marcus
Junius Brutus, one of Julius Caesar's assassins. Publius Valerius Publicola (d.
503 BCE) was a Roman consul, the colleague of Lucius Junius Brutus in 509
BCE, traditionally considered the first year of the Roman Republic; Livy,
History of Rome, 1.56–60. Dion of Syracuse (409?–354? BCE), the brother-
in-law of Dionysius the Elder, tyrant of Syracuse, became interested in
philosophy through study with Plato. Opposed to tyranny, he tried to set up
a moderate system of government with Dionysius the Younger as the model
prince; Plutarch, *Life of Dion*.

50. See Plutarch, *Life of Brutus*, 20–21, and *Life of Caesar*, 67–68.

51. La B seems to be referring here to the text in the Hippocratic Corpus
entitled *On Airs, Waters, and Places*.

52. Here, Artaxerxes, king of Persia in the fourth century BCE, who is said to
have offered great wealth to Hippocrates if he cured his soldiers of the plague.

that it would go against his conscience to be involved in healing barbarians who wanted to kill Greeks, and with his skills to be of service to a man who sought to enslave Greece. The letter that he sent to him can still be seen today among his other works and will forever testify to his good heart and noble nature. So it is certain now that, together with liberty, bravery is lost at the same time. Subjected people have no joy or keenness in fighting: they go into danger almost as if they were tied up and all benumbed, as if to pay their debt; they do not feel boiling in their hearts the ardor of freedom, which makes men scorn danger and want to acquire honor and glory by dying well amid their comrades. Among free men each vies with the others, every man for the common good, every man for himself. Every man expects to take his share of the evil of defeat or the goodness of victory. But enslaved men, in addition to this warlike courage, also lose their enthusiasm for everything else; their hearts are downcast and weak, and incapable of anything great. Tyrants well know this, and when they see this tendency in them they foster it, the better to soften them up.

Xenophon, a serious historian, of the first rank among the Greeks, wrote a book[53] in which he has Simonides speak with Hiero, the tyrant of Syracuse, of the woes of a tyrant: this book is full of good, serious admonitions, which in my view are as well-taken as can be. Would to God that every tyrant there ever was had set it before his eyes and used it as a mirror. I cannot believe that they would not have recognized their warts and been a little ashamed of their blemishes.[54] In this treatise he tells of the woes that tyrants have because, since they harm everyone, they are obliged to fear everyone. Among other things he says that bad kings use foreigners to fight wars and pay them, since they dare not put weapons in the hands of their people, whom they have wronged. (There have been good kings who paid foreign troops, such as in France itself, and more in the past than today, but with another intent: to hold onto their own people, since they considered the expense much less important than sparing men. I believe that is what Scipio, the great African, said: he would rather have saved one citizen than defeated a

---

53. The dialogue *Hiero*. See in particular 2.6–11, 4.1–5, and 5.1–3.

54. A curious phrase Montaigne repeats in "Vanity," III, 9. In praising the beauty of the city of Paris, he exclaims: "I love her tenderly, even to her warts and her blemishes"; Pléiade 1, p. 950; Pléiade 2, 1017; V-S, p. 972.

hundred enemies.[55]) But it is certain indeed that a tyrant never thinks that his power is secure until he has reached the point where he has no man of worth under him. Thus he will rightly be told what Thraso boasts of having reproached the master of elephants for in Terence:[56]

> You are so brave because
> You are in charge of the beasts.

But this ruse of the tyrants—turning their subjects into brutes—is nowhere more clearly recognizable than by what Cyrus did to the Lydians after he seized Sardis,[57] the capital of Lydia, and took the very rich king Croesus captive and carried him off with him. He was informed that the people of Sardis had revolted; he soon had brought them back under his power, but wishing neither to sack so beautiful a city nor to have the trouble of keeping an army there to guard it forever, he devised a fine strategy to secure it: he set up bordellos, taverns, and public games there, and published an ordinance saying the inhabitants had to patronize them. This "garrison" worked so well for him that he never had to draw a sword afterward against the Lydians. Those poor, miserable people spent their time inventing all sorts of games, so that the Romans made up an expression from them: what we call "pastimes" they called *ludi*, as if they meant "*Lydi*."[58] Not all tyrants

---

55. Publius Cornelius Scipio Africanus Major (236–184/3 BCE); Scipio the Elder defeated the Carthaginians at the battle of Zama (202 BCE), though Hannibal escaped, in the Second Punic War (218–201 BCE).

56. In the *Eunuch*, 3.1.414–15.

57. See Herodotus, *The Persian Wars*, 1.154–56.

58. This anecdote is based on Erasmus, *Adagia*, II 611 E–F, which in turn follows an etymology derived from Hesychius of Alexandria, a grammarian flourishing in the fifth or sixth century CE. The Latin word *ludi* means "games," "sports," or "pastimes," and *Lydi* refers to the Lydians (of Anatolia, the largest area of present-day Turkey); but it carries a potentially humorous note since the Romans also called the Etruscans "Lydians" because legend had it that the earliest Etruscans came over to Italy from the Asia Minor country. (A modern reader, too, might see some humor in "bordellos, taverns, and public games" as the "pastimes," or the *ludi*, Dutch historian Johan Huizinga refers to in *Homo Ludens* (1938); he theorizes that a society's culture resembles the characteristics of play, so there must be at least an element of play for a society's culture to develop.)

have so expressly declared that they wanted to unman their people, but in truth what this one ordained formally and openly most of them have pursued in secret.

In truth, it is in the nature of common people, whose number is always greater in the cities, to be suspicious of those who love them and gullible toward those who fool them. You should not imagine that any bird is more easily taken in by a decoy, or any fish swallows the hook more rapidly for an appetizing worm, than all people are quickly tempted into servitude by the slightest lure that is passed before their mouths, as they say; it is amazing how quickly they let themselves go if only you titillate them.[59] Plays, games, street-shows, spectacles, gladiators, strange beasts, medallions, tableaus, and other such merchandise were for people in ancient times the bait of servitude, the price of their liberty, the instruments of tyranny. Ancient tyrants used these means, these practices, these attractions to lull their subjects to sleep under the yoke. And so the besotted people, who admired these diversions, enjoying the gross pleasures passing before their eyes, grew used to serving just as foolishly—but more harmfully—than little children who are taught to read from seeing the bright pictures in illustrated books.

Roman tyrants devised yet another idea: frequent holidays for the public *decuriae*,[60] fooling that rabble—attracted more by gluttony than by anything else—as they needed. The wisest, most sensible man among them would not have given up his bowl of soup to regain the liberty of Plato's republic. The tyrants handed out a measure of wheat, a flagon of wine, a sesterce,[61] and then you should have heard people yell "Long live the king!" Those oafs did not stop to think that they were just getting back part of what was theirs, and that the tyrant could not even have given them what they were getting back if he had not taken it away from them earlier. The man who picked up the sesterce that day and gorged himself at the public feast, blessing Tiberius and Nero and their fine

[right margin, handwritten:] public festivals way to fool the populace into thinking king is generous

---

59. The following passage may echo Plutarch, *Moralia* 10 ("Precepts of Statecraft"), 802d–e, though the *Annals* of Tacitus would also offer considerable evidence about "the instruments of tyranny."

60. I.e., trade or craft corporations.

61. A Roman coin worth a quarter of a denarius (a silver coin), thus not a great deal.

generosity, would not utter a word, would not stir an inch, when he was forced the next day to give up his property to their greed, his children to their lust, his very blood to the cruelty of these magnificent emperors.

Common folk have always been like that: they are completely open to and corrupted by pleasures they cannot decently have, and insensible to the wrongs and pain they cannot decently tolerate.[62] Today I do not see one person who, hearing Nero mentioned, does not tremble at the very name of that ugly monster, that foul, filthy plague on the world. And yet it can be said that the noble Roman people felt such displeasure after the death (just as ugly as his life) of that arsonist, that torturer, that wild beast, remembering his games and feasts, that they were ready to go into mourning for him. That is what Cornelius Tacitus, a good, serious author, among the surest, wrote.[63] This will not be found strange, seeing what those same people had previously done at the death of Julius Caesar, who dismissed the laws and liberty: Caesar, a man whom I consider to have had nothing worthwhile (for his highly vaunted kindness did more harm than the cruelty of the fiercest tyrant there ever was, because it was that poisonous kindness of his that sweetened servitude for the Roman people).[64] But after his death those people—with his banquets still in their mouths and the memory of his lavish generosity in their minds— to honor and cremate him piled up all the benches in the square, and then raised a column to him as father of the people (as its capital had it); and they honored him after his death more than they rightfully should have done anyone in the world save perhaps the men who had killed him.[65]

The Roman emperors also did not forget as a rule to take the title of "Tribune of the People," both because the office was held to be holy and sacred, and because it was established for the defense and

---

62. This sentence's negative, "cannot decently tolerate," which Magnien makes to Smith's edition, is an important textual correction; see his *"Notes Additionnelles,"* p. 102; see Gontarbert's edition, p. 110.

63 See Tacitus, *Histories,* 1.4.

64. See Plutarch, *Life of Caesar,* 34, 46, and 48, concerning Caesar's "kindness."

65. See Suetonius, *Lives of the Caesars: The Deified Julius,* 1.84–85.

protection of the people.[66] And by this means, with the government's preferential treatment, they ensured that the people would trust them more—as if they should hear its name, but not feel the contrary effects. In our day, those who hardly do anything wrong, even something important, without preceding it with some fine words about the public welfare and general relief are not doing much better. For you well know, Longa,[67] the formulary[68] that they were able to use rather judiciously in some places; but for the most part there certainly can be no judiciousness where there is such impudence.

The kings of Assyria, and again after them those of Media, only appeared in public as late as possible, to make the populace wonder whether they were in some way more than human and to foster that illusion, about things they cannot judge by sight, in people who are prone to imaginativeness. Thus many nations that were under the Assyrian empire for quite a long time grew used to servitude with this mystery; and they were all the more ready to serve since they did not know what master they had, or whether they even had one, and they all credulously feared someone no one had ever seen.[69] The first kings of Egypt scarcely ever showed themselves without at times bearing on their heads a cat, at others a branch, at others fire, and they disguised themselves thus and acted like buffoons, and in so doing they inspired some reverence and admiration in their subjects by this outlandishness; whereas in people who were neither too stupid nor too enslaved, they would have aroused nothing but amusement and laughter, to my mind.[70] It is pitiful to hear

---

66. See Tacitus, *Annals*, 3.56.1–2; Suetonius, *Lives of the Caesars: The Deified Augustus*, 2.27.5.

67. See n. 23.

68. Apparently a reference to the *Preamble* to the *Edict of Fontainebleau* (1552), which dealt with King Henri II's reform of the judicial system. Despite the lip service it paid to the common weal, La B and others saw it as a hidden, venal attempt to fill the treasury's coffers in preparation for a royal visit to Germany.

69. In 1588 M noted that "[t]o preserve the authority of the king's council, there is no need for outsiders to take part in it or to see into it any more closely than from the first checkpoint. It must be revered with trust and in its totality if we want to foster its reputation." "The Art of Conversation," III, 8, Pléiade 1, p. 912; Pléiade 2, p. 979; V-S, pp. 933–34.

70. See Diodorus Siculus, *The Library of History*, 1.62.

of all the things tyrants of the past profited by, as a basis for their tyranny, and how many little things they made use of, because they always found the populace tailor-made for it. No matter how badly the net was cast, these people got caught in it; they always deceived them so cheaply that they never subdued them so well as when they were mocking them the most.

What can I say about another fine bit of humbug that ancient people took at face value? They were fully convinced that the thumb of Pyrrhus, the king of Epirus, performed miracles and healed diseases of the spleen. To enhance the story further, they claimed that after the dead body had been completely burnt the thumb was found in the ashes, still intact despite the fire.[71] Thus foolish people always make up lies themselves, and believe them afterward. Many people have written so, but in such a way that it is easy to see they have gathered it from city gossip and the populace's empty talk. Returning from Assyria and passing through Alexandria on his way to seize the empire at Rome, Vespasian performed miracles: he straightened the lame, he restored sight to the blind, and a whole lot of other fine things about which, to my mind, anyone who could not see the error in them was blinder than those he healed.[72]

Tyrants themselves found it quite strange that men could put up with a man harming them. They really wanted to get religion out in front of them as a bodyguard and, if possible, to borrow some spark of divinity to keep up their evil lifestyle. So Salmoneus, if we are to believe the sibyl of Virgil, in his Hell, because he had thus deceived people and tried to act like Jupiter, is now paying for it, and she[73] saw him in the depths of Hell,

> Salmoneus, suff'ring cruel pains, I found,
> For emulating Jove; the rattling sound

---

71. See Plutarch, *Life of Pyrrhus*, 3.

72. See Suetonius, *Lives of the Caesars: The Deified Vespasian*, 8.7.2, and Tacitus, *Histories*, 4.81–82. Vespasian ruled from 69 to 79 CE. La B may have sought to debunk Henri II's claim that he could cure scrofula with the "king's touch." Beginning in the thirteenth century, the miraculous power to cure scrofula, a form of tuberculosis affecting lymph nodes in the neck, was thought by many to be a special gift of French kings.

73. I.e., the sibyl.

Of mimic thunder, and the glitt'ring blaze
Of pointed lightnings, and their forky rays.
Thro' Elis and the Grecian towns he flew;
Th' audacious wretch four fiery coursers drew:
He wav'd a torch aloft, and, madly vain,
Sought godlike worship from a servile train.
Ambitious fool! with horny hoofs to pass
O'er hollow arches of resounding brass,
To rival thunder in its rapid course,
And imitate inimitable force!
But he, the King of Heav'n, obscure on high,
Bar'd his red arm, and, launching from the sky
His writhen bolt, not shaking empty smoke,
Down to the deep abyss the flaming felon strook.[74]

If someone who just acted the fool is treated so well down there, I think that those who have misused religion for evil are dealt with even more rightly.

Ours sowed some such things in France: the toads, the lily-flowers, the *ampulla*,[75] the *oriflamme* banner—as for me, I do not want in any way to misbelieve this, because neither we nor our ancestors up to now have had any opportunity to misbelieve it, since we have always had kings so good in peace and so valiant in war that, though they are born kings, yet it seems they were not made like others by nature but chosen before their birth by almighty God to govern and preserve this kingdom. And even if that were not

---

74. Virgil, *Aeneid*, 6.585–94, John Dryden translation. Salmoneus was a rash mythological king, the brother of Sisyphus, whose challenge to Zeus resulted in his being condemned to Hades. Magnien, in Tetel (ed.), *Étienne de La Boétie*, pp. 19–22, comments on these lines from the *Aeneid*, which Du Bellay also translated; in Du Bellay's translation, *Le Sixième livre de l'Eneide de Virgile*, they are lines 985–92.

75. A vessel filled with holy water used in the coronation of French kings. The royal emblem, or *oriflamme*, refers to a sacred red-orange banner that the Abbey of St. Denis presented to early French kings as their battle standard to inspire their soldiers. These items all figured in the "miracles" of King Clovis (461?–511 CE) of France, as described by the poet Ronsard in his epic *Franciade*, IV, 1143–1156—see n. 78.

so, I still would not like to take up arms to debate the truth of our histories or pick them apart in such detail: I do not want to take away the great fun that our French poetry—now not merely refurbished but, it seems, made completely new by our Ronsard, our Baïf, our du Bellay,[76] who thereby so advance our language that I dare hope that soon neither the Greeks nor the Latins will have any advantage in this regard over us, save perhaps the right of seniority—will be able to engage in so lustily. And I would certainly be greatly wronging our rhymes[77] (a word that I gladly use and I like, because although many have done it mechanically, I nevertheless see quite a few people who are capable of ennobling it once more and restoring its former honor to it) but, as I say, I would greatly wrong it now if I took away those fine tales of King Clovis, which I seem to see the talent of our Ronsard enjoying (with such pleasure!) so ably in his *Franciade*.[78]

---

76. Pierre de Ronsard (1524–1585), Jean-Antoine de Baïf (1532–1589), and Joachim Du Bellay (1522–1560). These poets were members of the group known as the Pléiade. Du Bellay's *Défense et illustration de la langue française* (1549), the group's manifesto, sought to establish French literary language as a worthy successor to Greek and Latin. From La B's poetry, it would seem he knew Baïf personally.

77. I.e., as opposed to "poetry," a distinction belonging to a tradition beginning with Aristotle's *Poetics*. It was part of the Pléiade's principles and assented to by M. Alluding to Horace and Seneca and praising Ronsard and Du Bellay, he asserted that "little beginners who inflate their words and marshal rhythms more or less like them . . . fall short of imitating the one's rich descriptions and the delicate inventions of the other"; see "The Education of Children," I, 26 [25], *Selected Essays*, ed. Atkinson and Sices, p. 66.

78. Ronsard's *Franciade*, a lyric epic history of France in four books along the model of Virgil's *Aeneid*, was long awaited by the poet's contemporaries (there were rumors about it as early as 1550), but it finally appeared in 1572, still incomplete. During the Renaissance several countries sought to trace their ancestry to the Trojans; Hector's son Francus was alleged to be the founder of France. In deference to Henri II, Ronsard alludes to Francus in his *Ode de la paix au roi Henri sur la paix faitte entre luy et le roi d'Angleterre, l'an 1550* strophes 3–6, lines 100–286. The treaty, known as the Treaty of Boulogne, temporarily ended the strife between France and England; Edward VI (1537–1553) was the nominal king of England though his uncle Edward Seymour, Duke of Somerset, was acting as regent when the treaty was signed. The next sentence implies a degree of familiarity—Ronsard may have known La B's poetry.

I understand his importance; I know the sharp wit, the grace of the man. He will make as good use of the *oriflamme* as the Romans did of their *ancilia*,[79]

> And shields thrown down from heaven,[80]

as Virgil says. He will deal with our *ampulla* as well as the Athenians did the basket of Erichthonius.[81] He will make our arms be spoken of just as well as they did of their olive branch, which they affirm is still in the tower of Minerva.[82] It would certainly be an outrage for me to try to contradict our books and thus intrude on our poets' game.[83] But to get back to the thread of my subject that I have somehow strayed from: to sustain themselves, tyrants have always striven to accustom people not only to obedience and servitude, but even worship toward themselves.[84] So what I have said up to now, about teaching people to serve more willingly, works for tyrants only with lower-class, common folk.

---

79. The Roman *ancilia* were small figure eight–shaped shields.

80. Virgil, *Aeneid*, 8.664. Legend had it that a shield came down from heaven into the hands of Numa Pompilius, ancient Rome's second king (717–673 BCE), thereby giving him divine sanction. He succeeded Romulus, Rome's legendary founder.

81. For the *ampulla*, see n. 75. In Greek legend, Erichthonius, an early mythological king of Athens, was the son of Hephaestus and Gaea, but was raised by Athena (La B refers to her as Minerva), who first had given him in a basket to a daughter of Cecrops, a mythical king of Athens who decided a contest between Athena and Poseidon to be the city's patron. See Apollodorus, *The Library*, 3.14.6.

82. See Pausanias, *Description of Greece*, 26–27. In the contest, Athena gave Athens an olive branch, which Cecrops thought was more useful than Poseidon's gift of a spring (producing salty-tasting water) because it provided oil, nourishment, and wood. See Ovid, *Metamorphoses*, 6.70–82.

83. "Game" in the sense of hunting wild animals; La B has no intention of meddling with the poets' "game" of depicting legendary history, which he considers fictitious, in their verse.

84. Although Machiavelli advocates using religion to control subjects, neither M nor La B does. At this point La B may have some of the more exaggeratedly flattering poems addressed to royalty in mind.

But now I come to a point that, to my mind, is the source and secret of domination, the basis and foundation of tyranny.[85] Anyone who thinks that halberds, guards, and watchtowers protect tyrants is quite mistaken, in my opinion. And I believe they are helped by these more as a formality and a bogeyman than for any reassurance they give. Archers keep badly dressed people who have no means from entering the palace, not well-armed ones who can carry out some action. It is easy to tally, certainly, that not as many Roman emperors escaped some danger thanks to their guards as were killed by their archers themselves.[86] It is not troops on horseback, it is not infantry companies, it is not weapons that protect a tyrant.[87] This will not be believed right off, but it is certainly true. It is always four or five who sustain a tyrant, four or five who keep the entire land in servitude to him. There have always been five or six who had the tyrant's ear, and have gotten there by themselves or else were called by him to be accomplices in his cruelties and companions in his pleasures, to pander to his lusts and share in the goods he pillages. These six manage their chief so well that, out of solidarity, he has to be wicked not only for his own wickedness but also for theirs. These six have six hundred who profit under them and they do with their six hundred what the six do to the tyrant. These six hundred hold under themselves six thousand whom they have raised up in state, to whom they grant either the governing of provinces or the handling of funds, so they will have a hand in their rapacity and cruelty and carry it out when the time comes, and otherwise do so much evil that they can only endure in their shadow, and be exempt from the law and punishment through them. Great is the following that comes after that; if anyone should wish to untangle this thread, he will see that not six thousand, but a hundred thousand, millions are linked to the tyrant by this cord, using it like Jupiter in Homer, who boasts that he will draw all the gods to himself if he pulls

---

85. See n. 11.

86. See Xenophon, *Hiero*, 3.8–9. M shares this view; see "Differing Outcomes from the Same Plan," I, 24 [23].

87. That a tyrant's military support is not the source of his protection is a Renaissance commonplace, but La B eschews the accepted tradition that his virtue is what secures him. The long passage that Tolstoy quoted, discussed in the Introduction, p. xliv, begins here.

Pyramid scheme of tyranny

the chain.[88] From this came the growth of the Senate under Julius Caesar,[89] the establishment of new posts, the creation of offices—all things considered, certainly not the reform of justice but new supports for tyranny.[90]

In sum, whether one gets there by patronage or sub-patronage, the profits of benefits one gains from tyrants, there are almost as many people whom tyranny seems to profit as those for whom liberty would be agreeable. Just as physicians say that once there is something wrong in our body, as soon as anything happens somewhere else, it immediately goes toward that sickly part: similarly, once a king has declared himself a tyrant everything bad, all the dregs of the kingdom—I am not saying a pack of petty thieves and jailbirds,[91] who can scarcely do either good or ill in a republic, but those marked by burning ambition and unusual greed—come together around him and support him, so as to get their share of the booty and be petty tyrants themselves under the big tyrant. That is what great robbers and famous pirates do: some scour the countryside, others ride after travelers, some lie in ambush, others keep watch, others massacre, others plunder, and although there is rank among them, with some as followers and others as heads of the group, still there is not one of them finally who does not have a share, if not in the main booty, at least in the hunt. It is indeed said that the Cilician pirates would never gather in such great numbers that Pompey the Great had to be sent out against them, but yet they drew into their alliance several fine cities and great towns in whose harbors they took shelter returning from their raids, and in compensation these were granted profit from fencing their plunder.[92]

---

88. See Homer, *Iliad*, 8.5–27.

89. See Suetonius, *Lives of the Caesars: The Deified Caesar*, 1.41.2. Julius Caesar was born in 100 BCE and was assassinated in 44 BCE.

90. La B may be alluding to abuses and injustices he attributed to Henri II, specifically in 1552 and 1554.

91. In La B's text, *essorillés*, or those who had had an ear lopped off in punishment for their crime, usually theft. The word was used to refer to any dishonest person.

92. See Plutarch, *Life of Pompey*, 24. Cilician pirates ruled the Mediterranean from the second century BCE until 67–66 BCE, when Pompey eradicated their influence. Cilicia corresponded to an area in southeastern modern Turkey.

The tyrant thus enslaves some of his subjects by means of the others, and is guarded by those of whom he himself ought to be wary if they were worth anything: as they say, to split wood he uses wedges of the wood itself.[93] So here are his archers, here are his guards, here are his halberdiers—not that they themselves do not suffer at times from him, but these poor souls, abandoned by God and men, are content to endure ill in order to do ill, not to the one who does it to them, but to those who endure it as they do and can do nothing about it.[94] Nonetheless, seeing those people who do the tyrant's business to profit from his tyranny and the people's servitude, often I am seized with astonishment at their cruelty, and sometimes with pity at their stupidity. For to tell the truth, what else is getting closer to the tyrant than drawing farther away from one's liberty and, so to speak, clutching servitude with both hands and embracing it? If they set their ambition aside a little and rid themselves of greed a bit, and then look at and really recognize themselves, they will see clearly that the villagers and peasants—whom they trample on as hard as they can and treat worse than convicts or slaves, although they are so maltreated—are, compared to themselves, still fortunate and somewhat free. The plowman and the artisan, though they may be enslaved, need not do any more than what they are told; but a tyrant sees the others near him cadging and begging his favor. Not only must they do what he says, but also think of what he wants—and often, to satisfy him, even anticipate his thoughts. It is not enough for them to obey him, they also have to please him, they have to break their backs, torture themselves, work themselves to death on his business; and then they must take pleasure in his pleasures, give up their tastes for his, force their character, shed their own nature; they have to be attentive to his words, his voice, his gestures, and his eyes; they should only have eyes, feet, and hands to look out for his wishes and to discover his thoughts. Is this living happily? Is this what you call living? Is there anything in the world less bearable than this, I am not saying for a stout-hearted or a well-born man, but just for one who has some common sense or merely the face of man? What condition is more miserable

---

93. A metaphor found in Erasmus, *Adagia*, LB II 70F–71A.
94. Tolstoy's quotation, beginning at n. 87, ends here.

than living this way, not having anything for oneself, owing one's well-being, liberty, body, and life to someone else?[95]

But they want to serve in order to have possessions: as if they could earn anything that belonged to them, since they cannot say that they belong to themselves, and as if someone could have anything of his own under a tyrant. They want to have the possessions belong to themselves, and do not remember that it is they who give him the power to take everything from everyone and leave nothing that can be said to belong to anyone. They see that nothing but possessions makes men subject to his cruelty, that no crime against him deserves death save that of the "wherewithal," that he loves nothing but wealth and despoils only the wealthy; and they come before the butcher to offer themselves up that way (fat and well-stuffed) and whet his appetite. These favorites ought not to remember so much those who have gained a great deal of property around tyrants as those who have amassed it for a while and then lost both property and lives thereafter. It should not come to their minds so much how many others have won riches, but how briefly they held on to them. If you study all the ancient histories and look at those of our own memory, you will see clearly how great the number is of those who, after gaining the ear of princes by wicked means, either making use of their wickedness or exploiting their naïveté, were destroyed in the end by those very men, and as easy as they found it to rise up, they then experienced afterward as much faithlessness to get knocked down. Certainly, among so great a number of people who have ever been close to so many bad kings, there have been few, or almost none, who have not experienced for themselves at times the tyrant's cruelty, which they had kindled previously against others. More often than not, after enriching themselves thanks to his favor with the spoils of others, they have ended up by enriching him with their own spoils.

Even upstanding people—if perchance any of them should be loved by the tyrant, no matter how far they advance in his favor, no matter how their virtue and integrity shine and lend some reverence for

---

95. M echoes these thoughts: "the greatest thing in the world is to know how to belong to oneself" in "Solitude," I, 39 [38], *Selected Essays*, ed. Atkinson and Sices, p 106; and "My mind is entirely its own, and is used to having its way" in "Being Presumptuous," II, 17, also in *Selected Essays*, p. 155.

themselves when seen from close up, even to the most evil men—I say even good, decent people nonetheless cannot not resist it, and must experience the common ill and themselves suffer from the tyranny. A Seneca, a Burrhus, a Thrasea,[96] that trio of upstanding men, the ill-fortune of two of whom even brought them close to the tyrant and put the management of his affairs in their hands, both esteemed by him, both cherished, and one of whom had even raised him and had his childhood upbringing as a token of his friendship—but these three, by their cruel deaths, testify sufficiently to how little certainty there is in the favor of an evil master. And in truth, what sort of friendship can be hoped for from one who is indeed so hard-hearted as to hate his kingdom, which only obeys him; and who, because he is not even capable of loving himself, impoverishes himself and destroys his own empire?

Now if one were to say that these men incurred such disadvantages because they had acted well, just take a good look around the man himself and one can see that those who came into his favor and remained there by wicked means did not last any longer. Who has heard tell of such unbridled love, of such stubborn affection; who has ever read about a man so obstinately passionate about a woman as that one was about Poppaea. Now she was poisoned afterward by the man himself.[97] Agrippina, his mother, had killed her husband, Claudius, to make way for him in the empire; to oblige him she had never refused to do or to allow anything. And so her very son—her nursling, the emperor she made with her own hands—after often failing her finally took her life, and there was no one then who did not say she had deserved this punishment all too well, if it had been at the hands of anyone else than the one to whom she had

---

96. Burrhus was Nero's preceptor; he and Seneca were in charge of the government during the first years of Nero's reign. Thrasea was a philosopher and Roman senator who refused to condone Nero's iniquities, beginning with the death of Agrippina, perhaps at Poppea's instigation, in 59 CE. These three "upstanding" men died between 59 and 66 CE, through the connivance or direct responsibility of Nero, who ruled from 54 to 68 CE. See Tacitus, *Annals*, 14.51, 15.60–65, and 16.21–35.

97. See Tacitus, *Annals*, 16.6; Suetonius, *Lives of the Caesars: Nero*, 6.35.3. Though pregnant, she died in 65 CE when Nero, in a fit of pique, kicked her not poisoned her.

given it.[98] Who was ever easier to manipulate, more naïve—to put it better, a greater simpleton—than Emperor Claudius? Who was ever more infatuated with a woman than he was with Messalina?[99] He finally put her into the hands of the executioner. If tyrants always have a weakness, it is not knowing what is the best thing to do. But somehow or other in the end, by dint of being cruel even toward those close to them, what little wit they have gets aroused. Typical is the comment of that other man who, seeing the uncovered breast of his wife—whom he loved best and without whom he did not seem able to live—caressed her with this pretty remark: "This beautiful head will be chopped off in a moment, if I so command."[100] That is why most ancient tyrants were usually slain by their greatest favorites, who knew the nature of tyranny and could not be as certain of the tyrant's will as they were distrustful of his power. And so Domitian was slain by Stephanus, Commodus by one of his own mistresses, Antoninus by Macrinus, and likewise almost all the others.[101]

That is certainly because a tyrant never either is loved or himself loves.[102] Friendship is a sacred name, it is a holy thing: it never

---

98. I.e., his life. See Tacitus, *Annals*, 14.1–13, and Suetonius, *Lives of the Caesars: Nero*, 6.34, who say Nero had her assassinated in 59 (CE).

99. Valeria Messalina (c. 17/20–48 CE) was the third wife of Roman emperor Claudius. She was also a cousin of Nero. A powerful and influential woman, with a reputation for promiscuity, she conspired against her husband and was executed when the plot was discovered. See Tacitus, *Annals*, 11.12 and 26–38; see 28.2 for "infatuated," *devinctum*.

100. Attributed to Caligula (12–41, who ruled from 37 to 41); see Suetonius, *Lives of the Caesars: Gaius Caligula*, 4.33.

101. For Domitian (51–96, who ruled from 81 to 96 CE), see Suetonius, *Lives of the Caesars: Domitian*, 8.17; for Commodus (161–192, who ruled from 180 to 192) and his mistress Macia, see Herodianus, *History of the Empire from the Death of Marcus*, 1.17; for Antoninus, known as Caracalla (86–161, who ruled from 137 to 161), see Herodianus, *History of the Empire*, 4.12–13 (although Caracalla was actually killed by a bodyguard, his assassination was apparently organized by his successor, Macrinus).

102. See Cicero, *On Friendship*, 15.52. In a tradition beginning with Plato, *Lysis* 214a and alluded to in the *Odyssey*, 17, 218, M frequently echoes La B on the exalted nature of friendship in "Friendship," I, 28 [27].

exists save between morally upright people[103] and stems only from mutual esteem. It is sustained not so much by favors rendered as by proper living.[104] What makes one friend sure of the other is the knowledge he has of his integrity: the guarantees of it he has are his good character, faith, and loyalty. There can be no friendship where there is cruelty, where there is disloyalty, where there is injustice. And it is conspiracy, not company, among evildoers when they assemble. They do not love, but fear, each other; they are not friends, they are accomplices.[105]

Now even if that were not an obstacle, it would still be hard to find assured love in a tyrant. For since he is above everyone else and has no companion, he is already beyond the limits of friendship, whose fair game is equality; which never hobbles, but is always even-gaited. That is why there is indeed some honor among thieves, so they say, in sharing loot, because they are equals and companion and if they do not love each other, at least they fear each other and do not want to weaken themselves by dissension. But those who are the tyrant's favorites can never have any assurance, since they themselves have taught him that he is all-powerful, and there is no right or duty obligating him; he grows used to consider his will as reason, and not to have any companion, but to be the master of all. And so is it no great pity if no one, seeing so many obvious examples and danger so present, wants to be wise at others' expense, and there is no one, among those so willing to draw close to tyrants, who has the presence of mind and boldness

---

103. La B's expression, *gens de bien*, is difficult to translate into English: it connotes moral goodness and uprightness, qualities La B indicates in lines 1–35 of his poem "Ad Michaelem Montanum"; for the entire poem, see Cottrell, "An Introduction to La Boétie's Three Latin Poems Dedicated to Montaigne," 26–29; see also pp. xlv–xlvii above.

104. See the passage in M's "Friendship," I, 28 [27]: "For just as the friendship I feel for myself is not enhanced by the aid I give myself when needed, whatever the Stoics say, and I do not feel at all grateful for any service I render myself; so the union of such friends, being truly perfect, makes them lose any feeling for such duties and to hate and avoid any words of division and distinction between them: benefit, obligation, gratitude, request, thanks, and the like"; *Selected Essays*, ed. Atkinson and Sices, p. 81.

105. See Sallust, *Jugurthine War* (*Bellum Iugurthinum*), 31.15 for the sense of "accomplices."

to tell them what the fox in the fable said to the lion who pretended to be ill: "I would be glad to go see you in your den; but I see so many animal tracks going in toward you, though not a single one coming back out."[106]

These wretches see the tyrant's treasures glittering and they are dazzled by the rays of his glory; lured by this radiance, they draw near and do not see that they are putting themselves in a flame that cannot fail to consume them. Thus the heedless satyr, as the ancient fables say, seeing the brightness of the fire discovered by Prometheus, found it so beautiful that he went to kiss it and was burned.[107] Thus the moth, hoping to enjoy some pleasure, flies into the flame because of its brightness but, as the Tuscan poet says, experiences its other power: it burns.[108] But still, let us say these favorites escape from the hands of the one they serve: they are never saved from the king who succeeds him. If he is good, they must at least acknowledge that they recognize the right. If he is bad like their master, he is sure to have his favorites, too, who generally are not content to take the others' place in their turn if they do not also have both their property and their lives, as a rule. So why should anyone, in such great danger and with so little security, want to take up the awful position of serving, at such pains, such a dangerous master? Good Lord, what punishment, what martyrdom is this? To spend one's nights and days trying to please someone and yet be more in fear of him than of anyone in the world, always to have one's eyes peeled, one's ears pricked up, so as to detect where the blow will come from, to discover ambushes, to sense one's companions' looks, to note who is betraying him, to laugh with each one and nevertheless be fearful of all, to have no one as either an open enemy or a sure friend, always keeping a smile on one's face and a chill in one's heart, not be able to be joyful and not to dare be sad.

But it is a pleasure to consider what they gain from all this torment, and what good they can expect for their pains and from their miserable lives. The people are all too ready to accuse not the tyrant, but those who control him, of the evils they suffer. These—peoples, nations,

---

106. A reference to Aesop's fable "The Sick Lion," though brought up by Plato, *Alcibiades* I, 123a, and alluded to in Horace, *Epistulae* I, 1.73–75.

107. See Plutarch, *Moralia* 2 ("How to Profit By One's Enemies"), 86f.

108. See Petrarch, *Canzoniere*, Sonnet 19, "*Son animali al mondo de sì altera.*"

beauty of the tyrant + also greatest danger

anyone at all, even peasants and plowmen—know their names, decipher their weaknesses, heap endless insults, endless contempt, endless curses on them. All their prayers, all their wishes, are against those men. They are blamed for all their misfortunes, all their plagues, all their famines, and if at times they do them some honor for show, even then they grumble against them in their hearts and feel a ghastlier horror for them than for wild beasts. This is the glory, this is the honor they receive for their service from the people, every one of whom, if he had a piece of their bodies, would still not feel satisfied enough, or relieved of their pains by half. But certainly even after they die those who come after are never so idle that the name of these "people-eaters"[109] is not blackened by the ink of countless quills and their reputation torn apart in countless books, and their very bones, so to speak, dragged by posterity, still punishing them after their deaths for their evil lives.

So once and for all, let us learn to do good. Let us raise our eyes to heaven, for either our honor or the very love of virtue, or certainly—speaking knowledgably—for the love and honor of almighty God, who is a sure witness to our deeds and a just judge of our faults. For my part I do think and am not mistaken—since there is nothing so contrary to a generous, kindly God as tyranny—that He reserves a place down there for some special punishment of tyrants and their accomplices.[110]

---

109. This word evokes Homer, *Iliad*, 1.231, where Achilles upbraids Agamemnon as a people-devouring king.

110. The concluding paragraph is reminiscent of the conclusion to Xenophon's dialogue discussing estate management, *Oeconomicus*, one that La B translated: "The gods . . . give . . . despotic rule over unwilling subjects to those whom they judge worthy to live the life of Tantalus, of whom it is said in hell he spends eternity, dreading a second death." (Loeb Classical Library, trans. E. C. Marchant, 1923, p. 525).

SUGGESTIONS FOR FURTHER READING

Sarah Bakewell, *How to Live, or, A Life of Montaigne in One Question and Twenty Attempts at an Answer* (New York: Other Press, 2010).

Robert D. Cottrell, "An Introduction to La Boétie's Three Latin Poems Dedicated to Montaigne," *Montaigne Studies* 3, no. 1 (September, 1991): 26–29.

Jean-Michel Delacomptée, *Et qu'un seul soit l'ami: La Boétie* (Paris: Gallimard, 1995).

Donald M. Frame, *Montaigne: A Biography* (New York: Harcourt, Brace and World, 1965).

Saul Frampton, *When I am Playing With My Cat, How Do I Know That She Is Not Playing With Me: Montaigne and Being In Touch With Life* (New York: Pantheon Press, 2011).

Floyd Gray, "Montaigne's Friends," *French Studies* 15, no. 3 (July, 1961): 203–12.

Olivier Guerrier, "Aux Origines du *Discours de La Servitude Volontaire:* Autour d'Un Mot de Plutarque," in O. Guerrier, ed., Moralia *et* Oeuvres Morales *à La Renaissance* (Paris: Champion, 2008), pp. 237–51.

James S. Hirstein, "La Boétie's Neo-Latin Satire," *Montaigne Studies* 3, no. 1 (September, 1991): 48–67.

Robert J. Knecht, *The Rise and Fall of Renaissance France, 1483–1610* (Oxford: Blackwell, 2001).

Robert J. Knecht, *The French Religious Wars, 1562–1598* (Oxford: Osprey, 2002).

Estienne de La Boétie, *De la Servitude Volontaire ou Contr'un*, edited by Malcolm Smith, with additional annotation and bibliography by Michel Magnien (Geneva: Librarie Droz, 2001).

Étienne de La Boétie, *De la servitude volontaire, ou Contr'un*, edited by Nadia Gontarbert, Collection Tel (Paris: Gallimard, 2005).

Étienne de La Boétie, *Discours de la servitude volontaire, ou Contr'un*, edited by Simone Goyard-Fabre (Paris: GF Flammarion, 1983).

Étienne de La Boétie, *Oeuvres complètes d'Estienne de la Boétie. Publieés avec notice biographique, variantes, notes et index par Paul Bonnefon* (Bordeaux: G. Gounouilhou; Paris: J. Rouam, 1892; reprinted Geneva: Slatkine, 1967).

Jean Lafond, "Le *Discours de la servitude voluntaire* et la Rhétorique de la déclamation," in Pierre-Georges Castex, ed., *Mélanges sur la littérature de la Renaisssance à la mémoire de V.-L. Saulnier* (Geneva: Droz, 1984), pp. 735–745; reprinted in J. Lafond, *Lire, vivre òu mènent les mots: aux formes brèves de la prose* (Paris: Champion, 1999), pp. 33–45.

Michel Magnien, *Etienne de La Boétie*, Bibliographie des Ecrivains Français (Paris: Memini, 1997).

Michel de Montaigne, *Oeuvres complètes*, edited by Albert Thibaudet and Maurice Rat, Bibliothèque de la Pléiade (Paris: Gallimard, 1962); cited in the notes as Pléiade 1.

Michel de Montaigne, *Les Essais*, edited by Jean Balsamo, Michel Magnien, and Catherine Magnien-Simonin, Bibliothèque de la Pléiade (Paris: Gallimard, 2007); cited in the notes as Pléiade 2.

Michel de Montaigne, *Les Essais*, edited by Pierre Villey and V.-L. Saulnier, augmented with a preface and supplement by Marcel Conche (Paris: Quadrige/PUF, 2004); cited in the notes as V-S.

Michel de Montaigne, *Selected Essays with La Boétie's Discourse on Voluntary Servitude*, edited and translated by James B. Atkinson and David Sices, with an introduction and notes by James B. Atkinson (Indianapolis: Hackett Publishing Company, 2012); cited in the notes as *Selected Essays*.

Nicola Panichi, *Plutarchus Redivivus? La Boétie et sa réception en Europe*, translated by Jean-Claude Arnould (Paris: Champion, 2008).

Richard L. Regosin, *The Matter of My Book: Montaigne's Essais as the Book of Self* (Berkeley: University of California Press, 1977), pp. 7–29.

François Rigolot, "Montaigne et la 'servitude volontaire': pour une interpretation platonicienne," in Iliana Zingner, ed., *Le lecteur, l'auteur et l'écrivain: Montaigne 1492–1592–1992*, Actes du Colloque International de Haïfa, April–May 1992, Colloques, Congrès, et Conférences sur la Renaisssance, no. 1 (Paris: Champion, 1993).

David Lewis Schaefer, ed., *Freedom Over Servitude: Montaigne, La Boétie, and On Voluntary Servitude* (Westport, CT: Greenwood Press, 1998).

Jean Starobinski, *Montaigne in Motion* (Chicago: University of Chicago Press, 1985).

Marcel Tetel, ed., *Étienne de La Boétie: sage révolutionnaire et poète périgourdin*, Actes du Colloque International, Duke University, March 26–28, 1999 (Paris: Champion, 2004). Tetel's book contains a number of important essays cited individually in the notes to this volume.

Roger Trinquet, *La Jeunesse de Montaigne: ses origines familiales, son enfance et ses études* (Paris: Nizet, 1972).

INDEX OF NAMES